Praise for Chrysal

"Virginia Woolf urged women to tell the truth about the body. Rosalyn Will, in *Chrysalis*, does this and far, far more. She shows us the grit and determination of how a woman who spent her early childhood during the Great Depression created a life for herself as a writer, while caring for herself and her family. This book is an inspiration to all of us who want to write our lives."

Louise DeSalvo, author of *On Moving: A Writer's Meditation on New Houses, Old Haunts, and Finding Home Again*

"With her clear gift for narrative, Rosalyn Will draws us into her story – the heartbreak of childhood; the pleasures of living and breathing and working and raising a family—all while enduring the difficulties of scoliosis. We read with rapt attention as her inner life unfolds and we salute her honesty, grace, and endurance."

Meena Alexander, author of *Fault Lines: A Memoir*

"At age 42 on exhibit for her untreated scoliosis condition in front of a phalanx of doctors, Rosalyn Will declares to herself that someday she is going to write a book. Lucky for us, at age 74 she has written that memoir. The cage of scoliosis is only one of the many cocoons we watch her struggle with and emerge from. Both in the detail and the breadth of this memoir, we are transfixed and inspired."

> **Nan Bauer-Maglin** co-editor, *Women Confronting Retirement: A Nontraditional Guide* and *Final Acts: Death, Dying, and the Choices We Make*

"Rosalyn Will has written an honest and engaging memoir of her fight to free herself from the restrictions of scoliosis and other afflictions of the body, mind and heart. This is a woman, and a work, of grit and compassion. You will like her plain style and real feeling."

> **Laurel Blossom**, author of *Degrees of Latitude*

Chrysalis: A Memoir

My Life

Beyond the Cage

of Scoliosis

Rosalyn Will

ISBN 978-0-557-48330-3

Grateful acknowledgment is made to the following publishers and authors for permission to cite from their works:

Bedford/St. Martin's for *America: A Concise History* Vol. 2 by James A. Henretta, David Brody, and Lynn Dumenil, copyright 1999 by Bedford/St. Martin's.

The Martindale Press for *Three Dimensional Treatment for Scoliosis* by Christa Lehnert-Schroth P.T., copyright 2007 by Christa Lehnert-Schroth.

Martha C, Hawes, Ph.D for *Scoliosis and the Human Spine,* copyright 2003 by Martha C. Hawes.

Joseph P. O'Brien, President and CEO of the National Scoliosis Foundation, for allowing me to summarize his introductory remarks at the 4th International Conference on Conservative Management of Spinal Deformities, 2007.

To my parents,

Syvila and Arthur,

who not only gave me life

but, by their example,

taught me how to survive.

To my husband, David,

who understood

my need to grow.

Contents

The cicada in the dark earth slept and grew,

Unknown to herself – no wing, no ray, no voice;

Until her seventeenth summer, blindly stirring

She crept and clung, moved by unquenched Life within her.

She grew and changed in the deepness of her being,

She grew and burst, and rent open her archaic shape,

Through the sore slowness, stepped out of herself and flew

To fill the bright air with a resonant song.

From "Beginnings," *Stepping-Stones of the Spirit* by Patricia Bever. Copyright, 1951, National Board of the Young Men's Christian Association (modified to reflect gender change)

Bone

David stares at the numbers where his thumb marks the measuring tape. "Sixty-two inches," he says, shaking his head. I asked him to measure my height because of what happened last night. He didn't question why. As he got the yellow tape measure from the kitchen drawer, I backed up to the wall where we've penciled the heights of our kids, and stood as straight as I could manage. Now he has me move away and then come back to be measured again. Again, the tape shows I am five feet, two inches tall. That's five inches shorter than when I married him in 1955.

I turn away, carrying the breakfast dishes into the kitchen. As they disappear beneath the sudsy water in the dishpan, I recall the strange disharmony of last evening; the way my body felt heavier, off-balance. Walking the few steps from counter to stove with the macaroni and cheese casserole was like moving through waist deep water. I promised myself an early bedtime, thinking I'd bounce back after a good sleep. David offered me the newspaper but I had no interest in reading it. I was too tired even to talk about our day, as we usually do. With our four children finally in bed, I wanted only to crawl into bed myself.

Slowly I got into my pajamas, anxious to stretch out. Turning down the covers, I found myself wincing as I pulled my legs up and eased my upper body down on the bed. But when I tried to stretch out, I couldn't. My spine refused to straighten all the way, even when I lay on my back. And when I turned on my side, my body curled toward a fetal position. Was it like this the night before? If it was, why didn't I notice? I recalled then that the previous week, the shopping bags I'd carried had been scraping on the ground. I thought King Kullen must have switched to longer shopping bags.

Five inches shorter. Centimeter by centimeter, during the fourteen years that I've been carrying and raising my children, I've been losing height, so incrementally that neither David nor I realized the full extent of it. I have precious little time to spend in front of a mirror. I'm thirty-seven, and still a naturally energetic person. Most days are so crammed with activity that I seldom give a second thought to my physical wellbeing. I tell myself that every mother feels occasional fatigue and pain.

The weight of the endless hours I spend doing what I need to do for my family seems to pull me down. I imagine these things are what any city housewife might do in 1970. On a typical day, I get three kids up and out to school; wash the breakfast dishes; bathe and dress the one-year-old; watch Sesame Street with him on my lap while I make a grocery list; carry the stroller down two flights; run up and grab the baby from his crib; run back down before someone takes the stroller (it's happened); go to the library, buy stuff for dinner; return home with child, stroller, books, and groceries, which requires three trips up and down; make lunch; rest a bit before three hungry kids come home; hear good days; hear bad days; rally myself to make meatloaf (flavored with ketchup because I forgot the onion); say "Hi" to my husband as he sits down with the paper; have a dinner table discussion about whether Agent 99 is smarter than Maxwell Smart on the Get Smart TV show; begin thinking whether we can afford to buy Eric a junior drum set for his ninth birthday; make sure Julie is settled with David to help her with math problems; wash the dishes; and put my youngest down for the night.

Now I understand that the scoliosis I thought had been arrested has been steadily weakening my body, worsening my curve. Fear claws my stomach, as it did when I was fourteen and first found out I had a problem. "Progressive" was the word the doctor used. "Scoliosis is progressive unless something is done to slow it down." I'd worn a brace until I was seventeen and assumed that had taken care of it. For several years after that, the small spinal curve they'd originally found didn't seem to worsen. I rarely thought about it. Or if I did, I literally put it behind me.

What could we have done differently? During the last several years of our marriage, David and I had sometimes talked about whether there was any medical option that might help. I figured it was too late for bracing, because my doctor had told me a brace is generally used to slow a curve in growing children. That would leave surgery. Even if all the expenses of an operation were covered by his insurance, who would take care of the kids while I was out of commission for weeks or months? There was no way our income could stretch enough to include child care. I don't remember exactly what we said during these conversations, but there never seemed to be any workable answers.

I struggle with shock, wishing that I'd wakened to the extent of the damage sooner. Now I've got to seek help. I must get a referral from my primary doctor in order to see an orthopedist.

A few days later, before I get an appointment, I'm on my way to the supermarket with my youngest laughing in his stroller. I'm wearing a soft, loose tweedy shirt and olive pants. The spring morning is so balmy, I'm thinking of taking the kids to the park soon for a picnic. Just as I turn onto the avenue, I hear a boy on the corner yelling. "Hey, hunchback!" His friends laugh and someone else joins in. "Look at her – she thinks she's somebody!"

Their words about my body strike my spirit; I whirl and glare at them. Then I realize what I've done: I've fallen into the trap of turning around when they named me.

Later, over a cup of tea, I sit thinking about these thoughtless children and how oblivious they are to the effect of their shouted words. It's taken me hours to sponge away their vocal graffiti; reminded me again of the fragility of my hope that others will see me as someone of worth despite my physical shortcomings.

And I have to wonder about how oblivious I've been. My awareness of having scoliosis has faded over the years because I still look normal from the front and feel physically strong. My curvature has become a benign presence that I gradually learned to live with. Now that it's grown worse, I can see it will sap my energy and threaten how I live my life. I must pay attention. How can I be a good mother if I get so exhausted? If I look bad to those kids on the corner, how do I look to my husband? The old fear of not being able to cope with things out of my control mounts in my gut.

At the same time, it is almost as if my emotional spine is strengthened by this old, this new, challenge. Maybe it's the caffeine in the tea. Or maybe I just decide to stop walking around with my eyes shut.

Thinking about my life up to now, I realize that ever since my diagnosis, I've worked hard at being an overachiever. I graduated from high school with honor in 1951, the first in my family to do so. Eighteen months later, I landed a copywriting job. By 1955, I had flown to Paris with my fiancé and started a new life in New York. I used to be able to make things happen. Though it seems lately that I've forgotten how, it has to be like knowing how to ride a bike, right? You don't forget. One of those kids was right this morning. I do think I'm somebody.

In the tiny change room at Columbia Presbyterian Medical Center, I leave my clothes in a heap, and think how curious it is that women my age were taught to cover themselves before all men but their husbands—except for moments like this – when their next-to-naked bodies must be put on display. The orthopedist appears kindly, with the studious air of a professor; a little overweight, balding, bifocal spectacles sliding down his nose.

Standing before him in the flimsy paper robe, I try to imagine how I look to him. A woman on the thin side, about 115 pounds. A woman obviously meant to be tall, but standing barely over 5 feet. Her legs are very long between hip and knee and again between knee and ankle, just like her mother's. Long arms end in slender `piano-player' fingers that seem to inch downward toward her knees. The middle of her body seems mismatched and thick, with a curious foreshortening of the trunk. At the doctor's request, she sheds the robe. His eyes move from the protruding breast bone just below her clavicle, to the long, once-flat diaphragm that is now creased in accordion folds under the pressure of a weakening backbone. Turning her gently around, the doctor's fingers trace the "S" trajectory of her spine, which has produced a considerable rib curve just below her right shoulder blade, and a lesser one near her left shoulder blade.

Sighing, he jots something on a pad and orders X-rays, and then continues his examination, asking penetrating questions such as if I've ever had polio (no). Finally, he tells me that most of the cushioning cartilage between my spinal vertebrae has deteriorated – it is simply gone. The doctor then surprises me by suggesting a newer kind of brace he thinks may help me. "I don't know how I can afford a brace," I tell him. "One of my four kids is a baby, so I can't work right now." "I'm going to send you to the Vanderbilt Clinic," he replies, "which is part of the Presbyterian Hospital– they have a sliding scale that helps people to pay –I think you'll find you can work something out with them."

Filled with hope and apprehension, I begin a series of low cost visits to the clinic, where I am photographed between neck and groin "for research purposes," and measured for a rigid plastic brace. I tell myself that it will help hold up my sagging body, although I remember vividly how uncomfortable even the more flexible canvas brace I'd worn in my teens had been. Will I be able to tolerate the shoulder to hip encasement of this more unyielding device? Can we afford to borrow the money to pay for it?

In June, I travel downtown to pick up the brace from the lab where it has been constructed. Looking from the address on a slip of paper in my hand to the number on the door, I stare at the name engraved above it: The Institute for the Crippled and Disabled. This is not me. I have never been crippled. Nor disabled. What am I doing here? I push the door open and step into a creaky elevator. Upstairs, I pay two-thirds of the reduced price of $200, which for us is still quite steep, and explain we will send the rest next month. All the way home, I pray that this expensive plastic cage will change my life.

This is it: Today I'm going to wear the brace for the first time when I go to the supermarket. That way I'll see how I function in it performing a routine activity. The technicians at the clinic had said it would be best to wear a t-shirt beneath it, especially on warm days like this one. As I fasten the brace firmly over the lower part of my body, I gasp at the discomfort I feel already from the metal piece that goes across my breast bone from one shoulder to the other. This seems to be the workhorse of the brace, which is probably designed to hinder the insistent curving of my body. But I have always been "chicken-breasted" so my breast bone juts forward right underneath the absolute rigidity of the crosspiece. It feels like someone is pushing me back toward the wall with a crowbar.

With all their measurements, why didn't they see that this would be a problem? Why hadn't they padded the crosspiece? Damn. My little son is all ready to go to the store, standing there in the playpen fussing to be taken out. I'll leave it on; maybe my body will adjust and it won't be so bad.

I make it to the store but can't wait to get home and take the thing off. The brace does hold me straighter than usual, but I doubt that I'll ever put it on again. My breastbone hurts constantly. I have a terrible time stooping to reach groceries that are on lower shelves. Even bending to pick up my son and settle him in the supermarket cart seat is an ordeal. I go back to the clinic, where they pad the crosspiece lightly with a thin layer of foam rubber. On my body, it feels exactly the same as before. The brace is consigned to the closet. And we still have to pay for it.

Five years pass; it's 1975. Desperate to discover some answer to my increasing discomfort, I turn to the Hospital for Special Surgery in New York, where I am asked dozens of questions, given breathing tests, and undergo a new series of X-rays. Now, on my return visit, the doctor sits, studying the sheets of film that show the alarming "S" that is my spine.

"You're forty-two years old, Mrs. Will. This is an advanced curve that you tell me started when you were fourteen, and except for three years of bracing at that time, has not been treated in any way. I am going to be very honest with you. At this late juncture, we would need to perform not one, but two operations, one going in from the front, and one from the back. It would be necessary for you to take time to recover after each one, so you'd be unable to work for several months. I am guessing that we could achieve only about twenty percent correction, which would still leave you with a sizable curve." After a beat, he adds, "There is a fifty percent chance that you might become paralyzed."

I had been expecting a tough diagnosis, some necessary pain and disruption. But two operations? Two recovery periods with no money coming in. And a high chance of paralysis. I try to process what he is, and is not, saying. His voice is quiet, almost apologetic. It is obvious he is warning me about the seriousness of taking such a step. Forget it, I know I should say. I tell him I want to think about it for a few days because a crazy thought hurtles through my brain: being laid up for a while would finally give me a chance to write. I'm a jug filled to bursting with a cork I can't seem to budge.

My brain struggles with this overload of stark facts and choices, none of which seem manageable. I get up wearily and turn to go. Gathering up my X-rays and chart, the physician asks if I would mind letting a few colleagues take a look at my untreated scoliosis condition. It seems a reasonable request; I know that this sort of information-gathering helps inform future understanding of difficult conditions. An aide takes me into a little booth where I remove all my clothing except panties. Instead of handing me a paper cover-up, she murmurs, "They're going to want to see you, dear," and smoothes small flesh-colored adhesive covers over my nipples. I'm going to be much more on display than I had expected.

When the doctor leads the way into the next room, I see that it is large, cold, and brightly lit. He indicates that I should step up on the slightly raised platform directly in front of us. There, to the left, are seated some twenty or so interns, clipboards in hand.

Now I begin to feel like a bug under a microscope, a damaged specimen on which to take notes. I had expected a smaller room and perhaps four or five interns with questions. Shivering, I remind myself that this may help them find answers for treating other people. But my body shrinks from having to appear in front of so many strangers. The chill of the room heightens the bluish pallor of the skin on my arms and legs. At the same time, ribbons of sweat run down my body. I fight the urge to turn and run. After a few remarks about my history, the doctor asks me first to turn with my back to the interns, then to walk slowly back and forth across the stage about ten times.

Overtaken by a mysterious calm, I begin to crisscross the stage, the doctor droning on nearby. I'm not sure what the people out there are seeing, but inwardly I reaffirm who I am and what this body and mind are capable of doing. I rise each morning, and get four children ready for the day. I make meals out of nothing and figure out how to make clothes last a little longer. Once, when I am seven months pregnant, I put down a new 9x12 shag rug, lifting the corners of the heavy sofa, so I can surprise David when he comes home from work. For years, I lug weekly loads of wash down two flights, across the courtyard in rain and snow, and down another flight to the basement laundry room. I create "Raggedy Ann" dolls out of saved bits of fabric and old nylons for my two girls. There are framed pen-and-ink sketches I've made of Gandhi and Schweitzer hanging on our living room wall. I write poetry in my head while I'm doing the dishes, and sometimes write it down. One day, I'm going to write a book. By the third or fourth turn, I walk with grace and dignity, and don't care what they are thinking.

When, in 1976, yet another medical consultant on scoliosis recommends either a dorso-lumbar (whole body) corset with steel stays in the back, or undergoing traction for two weeks in a hospital, I decide to opt out of this maddening search for workable answers to my problem. It's obvious that – at least for older women like me – there are none.

Around this time, I continue looking for clothes that fit my upper body loosely, yet are suitable to wear for work or church. This has been difficult because smock-like tops often are scarce or look like something to be worn at home, doing the cleaning. I've been making do for the last couple of years with two or three "big shirts," which actually were quite popular for a while, but I don't see them anymore.

One day, I walk past a Manhattan shop selling maternity clothes and notice a full-cut A-line jumper in the window. Just the thing, I think. Maternity clothing is always made with more room through the chest as well as the abdominal area. Shifting my bag to my shoulder, I step into the shop and begin to browse in the aisle where the jumpers are. Suddenly, I hear a female voice saying, "I'm going to have to ask you to leave, Madam." Curious, I turn to see to whom she is speaking. The woman is staring directly at me. Incredulous, I tell her that I probably will be buying a jumper, but need more time to look at colors. "I need you to leave right now." I stare back, alarmed at her hostility. "I'd like to speak to the manager, please." Thinking to settle this quickly, I follow her to the front counter, where a middle-aged man has just put down the phone. He turns and I see a coldness in his eyes. "This young woman has asked me to leave and I don't understand why. I have a back problem that makes it necessary for me to buy looser clothing, and I noticed the jumpers that you have in the…" The manager interrupts me curtly, and in an irritatingly bossy tone says, "I want you to leave right now. We sell clothing for young mothers—there's nothing here you would want." I am not only hurt, but angry. "It seems to me I should be the judge of that. I want to know why you are ordering me to leave." He never does give me a reason, and I turn to go because it's obvious that nothing is going to change. Decades later, the soreness in my heart remains.

In the early seventies I begin working part-time in the hosiery department of the new Gimbels East department store on 86th and Lexington. It's fun at first and gets me out of the house. But I'm increasingly asked to put incoming merchandise away, which involves bending and lifting. Within a couple of years, women's robes are added to the department just before Christmastime. As soon as the rush starts, I develop severe pains in my midsection. It's too high up to be a stomach ache, and I finally realize that with each robe I sell I'm bending down below the counter to get a big box to pack it in. Then I must lift and fold the garment – some of them heavy chenille or quilted cotton – to fit into the box. We're so busy taking care of Christmas shoppers that this happens every twenty minutes or so. My doctor tells me these are "arthritic pains" caused by the scoliosis, and prescribes a fairly strong painkiller. I hate the idea of taking pills for pain every day, and try switching to a low-rise girdle, which helps a little. Christmas is still weeks away. The pain persists. Finally, I ask if I can transfer to a different department where the merchandise is less cumbersome. In a few days I learn the transfer has been approved, but the personnel clerk looks at me apologetically. "I'm sorry. No transfers are allowed during the holiday season. Your new placement will be in fifth floor lingerie; it will begin after New Year's."

Although the transfer entails merely a physical move from the 'bargain basement' feel of the store's lower level up to the more attractive fifth floor, something unexpected happens: I find myself looking at everything through a different lens. I begin to examine the future and where I want to locate myself within it. I've had a lot of practice at this starting over business; maybe I'll get better at it.

I'm in my bedroom, standing in front of the old varnished dressing table that my parents have let me paint turquoise to match the new wallpaper. It's August, 1947, and I'm trying on the skirt my mother has just given me for my fourteenth birthday. A pretty girl with big brown eyes smiles at me from the mirror. Curly brown hair softens the face I've always thought too thin. My mother is standing in back of me, grinning.

I love this new skirt: black cotton dirndl, with ruffled tiers gathered under a four-inch elastic waistband. Each tier is trimmed with tiny, multicolor braid. I whirl around in front of the mirror, imagining wearing it to the next school dance.

Suddenly, my mother's long fingers encircle my waist and gently bring me to a stop. "Wait, hold still a minute." Patting my back on the right side just above my waist, she asks, "Is your blouse bunched up under the elastic? There's a lump over here." I feel around and am startled to discover the raised place she has touched. "No, it's not my blouse." I am mystified. Where would a lump come from?

I think frantically through the last couple of months. Did I fall in gym class when we were shinnying up ropes? No. Once, a boy pulled my chair out from under me when I went to sit down -- that was a long time ago. Lately, I've had lots of energy--I play tennis two or three days a week. Before school stopped for the summer, I was even getting better on the basketball team.

I used to be a picky eater. My mother got a terse letter from school saying I was malnourished. Furious, she went to the library for recipe books, and tried hard to get me to eat more. I remember her trying every which way to get me to eat eggs: finally she hit on the one I loved – eggs over easy on toast. But, since both my parents were on the thin side, it seemed natural that I'd be thin, too. I hated it when kids called me "skinny." Now, as a teenager, I can see that my lean frame is finally filling out, and my clothes look better on me. It seems ages that I've been waiting for the blossoming breasts my friends have. So far, only tiny buds have appeared.

But why a lump in my back? This is a mystery.

In 1947, I am five feet, six inches tall. Like other teenagers in the forties, I wear loose sweaters and blousy tops that don't conform to the figure. My mother has sort of Victorian ideas about what my sister and I wear anyway: she feels bodies are something to be covered up at all times. We don't look at each other's bodies, nor have much chance to study our own. Most of my friends, like me, grow up with cold bathrooms, so we bathe our whole bodies only once a week in the bathtub and wash briefly at the sink on other days. There is no lingering in a shower or inspecting ourselves in a full length mirror.

The next week I sit, for the first time ever, in an orthopedist's office. He pokes around the protruding place in my back and asks if anything hurts, which it doesn't. He asks me to bend over, sit, and walk. I remember getting more and more uneasy, wondering why they are making so much fuss over something that isn't bothering me at all.

Then the doctor asks me to go out in the waiting room so he can talk to my mother in private. This has never happened before. I pick at a loose thread in the upholstered seat of my chair. I sigh impatiently, fighting a rising wave of dread. When I've needed to see a doctor before, they would always just give me something to swallow or maybe smear on myself (like the calamine lotion when I had chicken pox). In a few days, I'd get better. I'd so hoped this visit would end with a simple solution, but now I don't think it will. I stare at a pile of magazines on a low table in front of me. But I don't feel like reading. I wish I were somewhere else. I wish I'd wake up from this really awful dream.

Through the frosted glass pane in the door, I see the doctor and my mother talking, but can't hear anything. When my mother steps out of his office, I don't like the way her face looks. Like it might crumple if she opens her mouth. She's avoiding saying anything, I sense, because there's nothing reassuring about what she has to tell me. Silently, we go downstairs to the street.

One of the favorite treats we share is going window-shopping and then to a restaurant for a sundae made with French vanilla ice cream and real, steaming, hot fudge. This day, after the doctor's appointment, we head straight for a restaurant about a block away.

My mother is very quiet, obviously mulling something over. The sundae tastes good going down, but there is a sour taste in my mouth. My stomach tightens as I wait for her to speak.

"The doctor says you have a curve in your spine called scoliosis. It feels to us like a lump, but he showed me how your spine is actually curving to the right side in that spot. Up by your shoulder blades, it's beginning to curve a little to the left. He can operate to correct it, but you'd be out of school for eight or nine months, and would have to stay in bed all that time in a plaster cast."

There, it's out. And now, it's inside me, reverberating down to the chill pool of fear. I gasp at the word 'operate,' but the thought of lying in a cast for months on end is awful, too. No tennis. No basketball. Hardly moving for days and days.

"I'm going to say 'No,' to the operation," my mother says carefully. She explains that she thinks it would be bad for me physically and emotionally to be nearly immobile and out of school for so many months. She has already asked the doctor what else we might consider. Now she emphasizes, "We have to do something because he says that scoliosis is progressive. We can't just leave it alone. It will get worse."

The relief I've felt momentarily at not having to face an operation quickly recedes. It will get worse. I struggle with this strange, new consideration in my life: the body that seemed to be growing stronger over the last few years is changing now in a frightening, perhaps uncontrollable way. I can't just take something to make this go away. What is going to happen to me?

Then, in a calm voice that tells me she is trying to reassure herself as well, my mother continues talking. She says that the doctor suggests, as an alternative, that I wear a brace. The idea doesn't appeal to me very much, but it offers a less frightening way to slow down the progressive curving of my spine, especially if I wear it until I stop growing, as the doctor has recommended.

Sitting there, surrounded by people relaxing with their afternoon tea and dessert, the whole thing suddenly becomes real. Swallowing hard, I fight the urge to start crying like a little child. What am I supposed to do with all this scary information? This isn't about someone else, it's about me. Stunned by the sudden change in my life from just a few days ago, I try to be calm and practical, like my mother. Still, a question pushes up from somewhere inside me and bursts out of my mouth. "Why is this happening to me—did the doctor say why?" "He doesn't know," she answers. "He said no one knows."

A week later, I stand stripped down to my underpants while a grandmotherly woman measures my torso for a canvas brace. It will have steel boning, she explains, like an old-fashioned girdle, and cover me from my shoulders to my hips in the back, waist to hips in the front. Straps made of heavy webbing (such as that used later for tote bag handles) will go over my shoulders, cross over in back, and be threaded through front buckles. This way I'll be able to tighten the brace around my body snugly to help keep the curve from worsening. Picking up a foam rubber pad, she says that there are many different kinds of curves; I have an S-shaped curve, so she must carefully decide where to put two pads in order to equalize the overall appearance of my back.

I remember the strangeness of that afternoon: my mother hovering and silent; I, hopeful but nervous; and the gentle, gray-haired woman who touches my body as if it were precious, as if it were beautiful. One part of my brain registers her kindness and the care she takes in preparing to construct the brace. The other part telegraphs shock as I stand before the wide, three paneled mirror, for the first time seeing my back as others see it.

Standing there nearly naked, I suddenly realize that, viewed from behind or from my right side, I appear crooked, misshapen. I never expected to be beautiful, but oh, I don't want to be ugly! I wonder if the brace will help me to be straight again.

The first day I wear the brace, we are in the middle of a warm and humid spell. Sighing with relief when I take it off that evening, I run a basin of hot, soapy water to soak the straps that go under my arms. It will be my job each evening to wash the straps, so that they will be clean for the following day. The whole corset feels damp and I'll hang it up to air, but it will get washed entirely only once a week because the heavy canvas takes so long to dry. We can't afford to have two braces made.

Gradually, I get used to feeling constricted and uncomfortable. Every night, on removing the brace, I see that the lateral straps and buckles that are tightened for support leave red welts on my thin body. They often cause numbness in my groin or pain over my hip bones. Still, I do feel straighter with the brace on, and the carefully placed padding helps to hide the irregular shape of my back. I tell myself I don't have to like it. It's just for now. Now lasts for the next three and a half years.

Today, I recall how sad and scary this time was for me. The diagnosis of scoliosis felt like a punishment, all the more because I had a guilty secret. When I was a little girl, one day I noticed pleasant sensations 'down there' while I was sitting on the toilet. Not yet seven years old, I had no idea of the connection between this and sexual arousal. Every once in a while I would explore with my fingers how to have that feeling again, and succeeded. I liked the way it made me feel – so I continued to do this off and on, right into my teen years. By then it was making me uneasy—I wasn't sure why-- but I didn't stop.

When the doctor said I had scoliosis, I wondered if God was punishing me. In our church, girls were taught that the body is a holy and inviolable temple; not only must we not allow a man to touch our 'private parts' until marriage, we were not to touch them ourselves except to keep our body clean. We were reminded that Eve gave in to the devil's temptation in the Garden of Eden; how she chose to disobey God's commands. As a result, Adam and Eve perceived their nakedness, fell from grace, and were forced out of Paradise. I felt that I had sinned, but I didn't have the comfort of confession that my Catholic friends had -- I was a Methodist.

I wish I could open up to my parents or sister about how it feels to be told you have a permanent condition like scoliosis. But how can I ask them to enter my pain? There is an unseen mourning going on within every member of my family as it is. From the time my sister and I were small, my mother has taught us not to talk to outsiders about family or personal problems -- maybe so we won't tell anyone that our father drinks. I learn to present a determined and cheerful face to the world. But it seems like my family never talks about really important things even in my own house. So, instead, I tend to focus on the practical necessities connected with the brace, and keep my feelings to myself. I'm not sure anyone is aware that there's this deep, sad longing inside of me, as if a close friend had died. In a way, that's what has happened: I am mourning the body I will never have.

Blood

Getting ready to leave home for good -- to leave Pittsburgh -- is harder than I thought it would be. I have a good job waiting for me in New York. But my mother has said she will send only one carton to me there. Today I must decide which bits and pieces of my former life to keep. Why? Will I become someone else in a strange city? It's hard to believe that I've just turned twenty-two years old. By any standard, I'm a grown-up. Right now, I don't feel like one.

Sitting cross-legged on the splintery attic floor, I open the few dusty boxes that hold my life up to the present. Beneath my high school diploma are clips of articles I wrote for three school newspapers going back to 5th grade. Some scribbled poems fall out of dog-eared black and white Mead notebooks, and I tuck them into my `save' box. I take the citation that says I have won the 1949 Pennsylvania School Press Association's First Prize in Poetry for "The Endless Search." I rescue the crayoned picture of the Italian ice vendor who stopped outside our junior high school on warm days. Inside a large envelope is a picture of me in my white eyelet, junior high graduation dress. It's a profile shot and my arms are carefully positioned to hide my back. There are many childhood photos, but few show our small family all together: my mother, father, sister, and me.

One photo slips from the pile that I sort through: I pick it up and study it, realizing that it's a faded snapshot of my father's first family—the three children that have grown up without him. Strange, isn't it? I've spent half my life not knowing about them and the other half, questioning why they aren't part of our family.

According to my sister, who finally filled me in when I was eleven, my father married my mother after the death of his first wife left him with three kids under four years old. Their mother died when she was only twenty-one years old -- from peritonitis, a severe infection that set in after her appendix burst. Not knowing what else to do, my father took his children to stay with their maternal grandmother for a while.

But a few years later, when my father asked my mother to marry him, she was twenty-eight years old, used to being independent and unburdened. Did she feel put upon, being asked to raise another woman's children? Or was she unsure of her child-rearing skills? Whatever her reservations, she made it clear from the beginning that she wasn't willing to take on a 'ready-made family.' He apparently continued to hope she would change her mind. She didn't.

My father's first family grew up motherless and fatherless, raised by a loving grandmother and an aunt in Kentucky. My sister and I grew up in Pittsburgh, Pennsylvania. The family didn't exchange letters or gifts with them, although my father stayed in touch by exchanging occasional notes and photographs.

At eleven, my feelings of allegiance were switching to my mother. My father was drinking more around this time. My mother was the sane and stable one. I thought she'd been wrong to deny him his family, but at least she did tell him her feelings before they were married. Why did he go ahead and marry her? Why had he expected her to change her mind? I was beginning to understand her rebellion at being put in the strict wife/mother box of the time. What I still didn't recognize was the prison of pain and regret my father lived in. His method of coping with his separation from his other children was spending more time in the bar across the street. That didn't help me to understand; I didn't like who he was when he was drinking and started to turn against him.

The August sun is higher in the sky and the attic has grown unbearably hot. I quickly close up the `save' carton and drop the photo of my father's kids back into the envelope of pictures I'm not taking. I don't expect to see them again anyway. Glad to leave behind the stirring of memories that evoke both anguish and puzzlement, I find myself walking as I have so often, to the edge of Mount Washington, just a few blocks from our house.

I pass Knells' bakery, where I used to buy day-old cracked wheat bread for nine cents a loaf when we lived on Shiloh Street in the early forties. There's the A&P I went to for my parents' favorite Maxwell House coffee, breathing in the wonderful aroma as fresh beans poured into a grinder and filled the bright red bag before my eyes.

From the corner of Shiloh and Sycamore, I can see down the street to the Methodist church I've grown up in. There it sits, planted firmly right next to the Baptist Church, co-existing in gentle rivalry for who knows how many years. I pause, recalling the day `Uncle' Jim Johnson wasn't there to lead the singing in Sunday school. My hand flew up so fast when they asked for a volunteer, I didn't have time to be afraid. I was fifteen years old, not knowing what I was doing, but trusting the singing Methodists not to let me down. All I had to do was get them started. The audacious sound of my own voice leading off was quickly joined by the strong voices of 50-odd people who grew up believing that singing was a form of worship. They loved doing it. The harmony was rich and full, especially when we got to the chorus: "When the roll, (`When the roll,' roared the basses), is called up yonder…" The sound of those voices, and those of my mother and Aunt Nell at the piano after supper, formed a deep well within me that I revisit when my spirits need lifting.

I cross Grandview Avenue and stand at the edge of the mountain. Tall old trees wrap me in blessed shade as I look out at the city I'm already beginning to miss. There are weeds along the iron fence, but beyond and down the hillside, a vast metropolis is reinventing itself. I think of the countless times I have stood in this very spot: on hot days like this one when I am seven, and come home with swelling mosquito bites on my ankles that later get infected. On a crackling winter night when my mother walks over with us to see the dazzling panorama of city lights that are so seldom visible.

From the age of two, I have grown up on this mountain, 500 feet above the city. For months at a time, though I might stand at the fenced rim of the mountain, I can see nothing. Before the development that eventually transforms this part of the city into The Golden Triangle, a sparkling complex of corporate headquarters, public parks, and upscale hotels, Pittsburgh's burgeoning steel industry renders it a city of smoke.

As a child in the thirties and forties, I often walk several blocks on Grandview Avenue to borrow books at the library. Standing by the fence, though I peer intently over the hillside, I feel completely shut off from what I know is there. Great gray clouds of roiling smog lie between me and the Smithfield Street bridge where cars creep at noon with their bright lights on; between me and the tug boats, the river barges, the vast expanse of the Monongahela River itself. Only on rare days is it possible to see where that river joins the Allegheny, forming the point of the triangle, and flowing on into the Ohio. At seven or eight, the feeling of being encased in a cocoon is strong.

At first, I like this fogged-in feeling; I'm in a special world, where everything outside seems muffled and non-threatening. Even the angry looks my parents exchange at the dinner table. Even the war in Europe.

The world seems to become a more dangerous place when the Japanese bomb the U.S. base in Pearl Harbor, Hawaii. It happens in late 1941, and soon after, the United States enters World War II. In school our teachers pass out little pamphlets with silhouettes of enemy planes, and tell us we should learn to identify them. At home, we're required to install heavy black air raid shades to block light from showing at our windows. Air raid drills become a regular fact of life. My mother goes to the store now with her ration coupon book; meat, butter, sugar, coffee, and chocolate are severely rationed. She comes home with anemic white oleo in a plastic bag, and kneads in a capsule of coloring that makes it look like butter. There's a big difference in taste, but it's better than nothing. That winter my sister and I build snowmen we call Hitler and Hirohito, and throw snowballs at them till they fall over.

My parents don't fight as much as they used to but the air often buzzes with tension. No one ever gives anyone a hug. I need a warm, safe space in which to burrow, a hideaway where I can learn to not be a little kid anymore. I can't always visit the clouds of smog that inhabit the river valley to help me imagine a different reality. In time, I discover it's possible to disappear into books instead. But while other children are learning how to interact in everyday situations, most of my childhood is spent inching toward normalcy. Classmates see me as a lonely, socially inept child, skinny and shy. They regularly let me know that they are normal, and I am different.

Our family's social isolation troubles me even more as I grow older and begin to question. I don't understand the separateness that manifests itself in so many ways -- both within, and outside my family. Why don't we ever visit the homes of friends? Why don't any friends come to visit us? We have close relatives in Pennsylvania, but never see them. I finally meet my mother's brother when I'm a teenager. [Many years later, I will discover that my father had a younger sister with twelve children. She saw his death notice in the paper.]

Growing into adulthood, there is so much that puzzles me. I need to know more about what's going on out there in the world. I already see that many other families don't live in the isolation that seems to be our norm. I want to know more about what is *in* there, too, deep within my own family background, another area completely hidden from view. As a young teenager, I talk to my friend, Emmy, all the time about the strange climate at home. One day we stand right where I'm standing now, looking out at the smoggy carpet, both of us crying about the latest fight our parents had. It helps to confide in one another, but neither can help with the other's questions. The thick clouds surrounding my parents' marriage create a fog of secrecy and guilt that I am still trying to penetrate.

There have been few clues along the way: unfamiliar names mentioned in my parents' conversation: Aunt Cece, and Smitty, referred to as "the black sheep of the family." And then, what my sister tells me, on an unusual evening when both our parents are out of the house.

It is 1944, she's sixteen and I'm eleven. Suddenly, the quiet is punctured by the local air raid siren emitting its undulating wail. She scrambles to pull the black shades down over the windows while I turn out unnecessary lights. We are used to the drill by now, but somehow there is a heightened sense of drama in the darkened rooms. My sister feels it, too, and her voice drops, as we are talking, to a confidential tone.

"I don't know if I should tell you this, but Mother told me the other day that she hadn't wanted a second child. She was pretty unhappy when she found out she was going to have another baby."

I don't remember feeling particularly upset as I took in this information, as though it had nothing to do with me personally. I seem instead to recall, as the steady all-clear siren sounded, somehow feeling grown-up because she had chosen to share this with me.

Why did she, I wonder now? Was she feeling vulnerable and wanted me to feel vulnerable, too? Did it occur to her then, as it has to me much later, that our mother may not have wanted any children, including the first one?

When we raise the blackout shades, the air has grown charged and heavy. Lightning rockets across the sky. I've never been afraid of storms, but as the rain pours down and thunder booms along the hills, I suddenly sense how it might be if those sounds were bombs, if it were tracer bullets lighting the underside of clouds. The war, which has always seemed distant, now becomes real, immediate, happening on my own street. I turn quickly away from the spattered window, wondering what prompted my sister to tell me I'd not been wanted. I know she's been having a hard time in high school lately and has a teacher she doesn't like. Her grades are slipping while mine are doing okay. Our mother is often cross with her, not understanding why she can't do better. One day I heard her say, "You're the oldest. You should be setting the example." Maybe that is why.

When the stock market crashes in October, 1929, my father is immediately laid off. He's handy with tools and learns quickly how to run machinery, so he tries to pick up temporary jobs. But who has money to pay him? What happens when his money runs out? There are city relief agencies, but a man has to prove that he hasn't worked in months. At that time, there is no such thing as federal unemployment insurance.

By 1931, the mood in Pittsburgh is one of desperation. Many people have overused credit, spending far more than they can earn; even those with savings suffer when 130 banks collapse. Three years later, a good third of men ready to take any kind of work can't find a job. Thousands of working class families find themselves in deep financial trouble. Some become homeless and dependent on strangers for food.

Deep in my memory is the haunting image of a man who knocks on our door and asks if he might do some work in exchange for a sandwich. His shoulders sag. He looks as though he's been walking for hours. But it is his eyes that I particularly remember: they are full of hurt and astonishment – how is it possible that he is begging for a meal? When my mother hands him a baloney sandwich and a cup of steaming coffee, she tells him to rest a bit. He sits outside on a step, fighting tears before he can begin to eat.

When my father is out looking for work, he sees these men lining up for handouts of apples or bread, and worries that soon -- with a wife and two children -- he may be one of them. For men like him who fought in World War I, there is no "GI Bill." Not even a one-time cash award. Nothing at all from the government to enable a returning veteran to get more education or buy a house—like the generous allowance that will be given to millions of World War II veterans in the mid-forties. His sixth grade education and meager odd-job work experience don't help him compete with other semi-skilled men desperate for work in the mid-thirties. His previous jobs have all been low-paid, and none lasted longer than two years. My mother is good at managing money, but she, too, is under pressure. My father feels helpless, and when he feels helpless, he drinks. And then they fight.

Born in 1933 at the height of The Great Depression, I am two years old when we move to the Bigham Street house on Mount Washington, the first house I remember. Though future city planning will completely transform the decaying city triangle below the mountain, in 1935, it isn't golden yet. Very early I sense a gloominess that seems to settle over everyone and stay there a long time. It has something to do with money. Every so often, my mother gets out an old teapot and recounts the coins she's managed to put away. She saves string from the butchers' and makes note pads out of cut-up sheets of paper with writing on one side. My father cleans bacon grease from the heavy iron skillet with crumpled newspaper to save on soap and paper towel. We kids know not to ask for anything new.

Our family lives in a rented house that has two bedrooms, but no central heating. On frigid winter mornings, my sister and I, watching our breath condense in the bedroom air, crawl out from under our heap of bedclothes and run downstairs to the living room. There we jump up onto the scratchy horsehair sofa that is set before a blazing fireplace. Our mother has our clothes waiting for us, already warm from the fire. Shivering, we race each other to get dressed. Until we get the last sweater and woolen stockings on, the back half of us has goose bumps and the front half feels scorched.

In warmer weather, I spend endless hours on our 'screen-porch,' a latticed room that lets in squares of sunlight and perfumed air, and shelters me from all but the heaviest rains. There's a comfortable old wicker chair with a cretonne-covered pillow where I sit and talk with my dolls. Sometimes my sister and I sit cross-legged on the floor playing games. In the corner by the kitchen door stands the ice-box, supplied twice a week by a big guy in bib overalls who uses tongs to hold huge blocks of ice on his padded shoulder. In the really warm weather a box with the newest kittens might be out there. I long to put one in my lap to pet, but I know that they are babies and must be treated gently.

The smells of earth and growing things make the screen-porch a comforting place, which is why I take refuge there when my parents are arguing. I'm too young to understand most of the words they use, but my mother seems close to tears and my father gets all red in the face. Once, my mother is ironing when the conversation suddenly becomes a shouting match. From the doorway, I watch as she faces my father across the ironing board, only inches apart. I wonder if she will drop the hot iron or maybe even throw it at him. No. Some cool part of her turns off the iron, and sets it down on its metal plate. Then, she hurries out from behind the ironing board and the two of them march upstairs to their bedroom and slam the door. They always do that when their fighting gets loud.

Maybe they think that is better than having their children see them out of control. But when they are shut into the bedroom, we don't know what's happening. Though I am still downstairs, the waves of their anger break over me like blows, engulfing me. Their voices go up and down, muffled hammers of accusation and denial.

I have trouble remembering the last time they laughed together at silly things. I am sad that they are different people when they fight. Worst of all is wondering each time how it will end. What will happen next?

Years later, my sister laughingly tells me that, sometimes, I would run into the living room and put my head under the sofa pillows so I couldn't hear them. I stare at her, wondering why she thinks it's funny. It was never funny. What I recall is that my apprehension began to translate into frequent colds and in between them, I'd nervously cleared my throat every night before I fell asleep.

Somewhere in the mid-eighties, I travel back to Pittsburgh and stand once more on Bigham Street, looking at that first house. It appears so much smaller now that I am bigger, a simple frame house with a pitched slate roof and slightly sagging front porch. I stare at the molding around the roof, the plain wooden frame around the front door, searching for the ugly images of gargoyles. But the gargoyles in my memory are of a different sort.

In a poem I write thirty years after leaving that house, I speak of them as not only present, but alive:

> How I must have dreaded at three or four
> That shadowed porch with gargoyles at the door.
> I stood unsmiling, staring down the years,
> Feeling how their weight had hollowed me.
> I turned to go. The gargoyles followed me.

Memories of what went on during the five years I lived in that house are like the oldest of early films—quick, flashing, black-and-white images: slammed doors, angry eyes, grim mouths. Then, there was the silence. Silence in the kitchen, silence at the dinner table, sudden silence when we children walked into the room. What is one to do with the memory of faces closed upon pain, the refusal -- or maybe inability -- to get out jagged things and talk about them so that they don't hurt so much? Decades later, I see myself as a young child, chilled by my mother's taut mouth while she stirs the oatmeal, my father's tense shoulders as he stares out the window. Their silence is thick and deep as my sister and I try to eat our breakfast. Our spoons click loudly; our chewing and swallowing echoes in our ears. In every photo taken during those years, I stare solemnly into the camera. I think now that the silences were so profound because each of my parents had dreams and expectations that never came to fruition.

Sometimes, after an argument, my father storms down the stairs and out the door. He comes home long after I am asleep. The next morning my mother moves zombie-like from stove to table. She says nothing. My father eats quickly and heads for the back yard, where his square-framed black Model A Ford sits, solid and nonjudgmental. He slides into the driver's seat but doesn't start the car. Removing himself from the likelihood of more argument, he lights a hand-rolled cigarette and sits there quietly, reading a Zane Grey western.

My father is brown-eyed, curly-haired, tall and handsome. His natural inclination is to gentleness, openness. He sits me on his knee and sings nonsense songs to me:

"Oh, it ain't gonna rain no more, no more,
It ain't gonna rain no more,
How in the heck can I wash my neck
When it ain't gonna rain no more?"

If I hurt myself, he picks me up, lets me cry a while and then says, "You all done crying now? Good little soldiers don't cry. You want to be my good little soldier?" This makes me feel proud; I stop crying and smile at him.

I think now that he found it easier to be a good father because he'd had experience with his other children, the children of his first family.

While I watch my father sitting in the car through the screen door, my mother is inside, working out her anger by cleaning drawers and cupboards, or washing clothes in the old wringer washer that she has to crank. She works herself to exhaustion to keep from exploding. Or is it that housework is something she is able to control?

My mother is tall and wiry, with startling blue eyes. Her straight dark hair is long enough to sit on, but she keeps it tidily braided and pinned up on her head. Though she seldom talks to my sister and me about her younger days, we know that our mother was raised in Glenwillard, Pennsylvania. During her growing up years, she spent a great deal of time at worship and social events in a nearby Methodist Church. The few photos that remain show her outdoors with friends, often around rowboats and water in summer, or looking fresh from a snowball fight in winter. In her twenties, she dresses in white shirtwaists and middy blouses, checked or plaid mid-calf skirts, a swashbuckling winter coat with fur trim at the neckline. One picture shows my mother wearing forbidden knickers at a picnic. She had to smuggle them out of the house in a bag because her parents thought only "fast" women wore them.

Years later, when I am ten or so, my mother invites me into the middle bedroom. My parents' bedroom is usually off-limits to my sister and me. Something about her face looks different to me, softer, as though she has a happy secret. I watch as she stands on tiptoe, lifts a large cardboard box down from the highest shelf in her closet, and sets it down between us on the bed. Curious, I wonder if the box might hold hand-me-down sweaters from my sister. I hope not, they're never the right color for me.

When her long graceful fingers remove the lid, the room slips away. We sit on her bed, on a day that does not appear on any calendar, and go through her single box of keepsakes. She spreads out pencil drawings of wild horses at a gallop, their manes flying. I look up in surprise; she smiles and nods. Not once have I ever seen her sketching. Then she turns over a large old-fashioned photographer's folder; inside, a beautiful young woman with challenging eyes and long hair falling down in ringlets: my mother, at nineteen. My mother, as I have never imagined her.

There are more photos: rigidly formal ones of her older brother and sister: he in World War I uniform and posed with a guitar, she in a ruffled dress, looking properly modest. I finger a fragile autograph book that belonged to my mother's mother. It is dated 1885, and overflows with the spidery writing of long-ago friends.

Rain beats on the windows. My mother switches on the bedside lamp. We laugh over yellowed newspaper ads from the 1920s selling fashions cut long and straight, all the rage in the flapper era, but looking odd in the forties. She tells me of a year when "apple green" was the new spring color. She bought a dress in that shade. "I looked awful in that dress, and never wore it!"

Leaning forward, I see that we are almost to the bottom of the box. There is an old shorthand textbook and a few of her practice papers; several faded photos of her with young men not my father. Nothing else. I wonder if she has a different box for keepsakes from after she was married.

I still cherish the warmth of that afternoon. There would be only two or three other times like it when I was able to feel that close to her. I remember wishing that the box's contents were endless. Here were the only clues I had to the person she had been before she was my mother.

It would be a long time before I understood that, with marriage and motherhood, she had felt forced to become someone else. Housework bored and frustrated her. She wanted so much more than that, but there was no Betty Friedan for women of her generation. I think now that she would have been so much happier out earning a salary, as she did before she married. But after the 'Rosie, the Riveter' boom during the World War II years, the women who'd filled empty factory jobs vacated by men were sent back home. Their role -- according to the times -- was to cook, clean, and care for the children, not take jobs away from men, who were the traditional family providers.

The mood in our house, as in the country, gradually brightens once President Roosevelt's New Deal reform programs go into effect. The Social Security Act for the first time provides a system of unemployment compensation, and guarantees pensions to people over age 65. The Works Progress Administration (WPA) puts out-of-work men on the federal payroll, renewing infrastructure and public buildings. These are the kinds of hard manual labor jobs my father has experience with; this legislation may be what saves our family from economic ruin.

Slowly, the thing we've been sorely missing – hope – comes back into our lives. My mother takes me to the music section in a downtown five-and-ten, where a pianist is belting out the popular tunes of the day. We stand and listen for a while and then she spends a dime or so on sheet music to take home. Because we can better afford trolley fare now, we take trips to the Phipps Conservatory filled with sweet-smelling blossoms, and spend time in Carnegie Museum, awestruck by the gigantic skeletons of dinosaurs. Every Saturday morning, my mother gives my sister a whole quarter, enough to get both of us into the movies, and a bit of penny candy sticky-sweet in our mouths. We sit, blissfully rich, through a double feature, cartoons, and a weekly "Perils of Pauline" cliffhanger serial.

Before the end of the decade (1940), my father finds a permanent job with a public utility, maintaining and monitoring gas pressure gauges. Working for a utility is a godsend--people are always going to need light and heat. Despite my father's other problems, this is the job he will have for the rest of his life.

Now there begin to be more smiles in our house and not so many arguments. We sit around the living room in the evening listening to the goofy antics of Fibber McGee and Molly, or Jack Benny, on our Philco radio. I often sit cross-legged on the floor by my mother's chair while she absently lets her fingers play through my hair.

These are the years when housewives across the country are eagerly addressed by "women's magazines," Ladies' Home Journal, Woman's Home Companion, and Good Housekeeping –every one of them edited by a man. They feature advice columns, recipes, beautifully illustrated fiction, and advertisements.

My mother gets the idea from an article on healthy posture that we kids should practice walking carefully around the border of our old red carpet, backs straight, balancing a book on our heads in order to improve our posture.

Looking back, I wonder if we'd kept it up, whether things would have turned out differently for me.

Unfortunately, we circle the carpet every night only for a few weeks. Many evenings, we lose track of how many times we've gone around because the books keep falling off our heads and we all end up laughing. The laughter is good; it fills up some part of me that has felt starved.

While we are still at Bigham Street, for Christmas one year, my father makes us a little wooden "kitchen cabinet" painted a shiny brown and my mother stocks the shelves with miniature dishes and pots and pans. Our house is so small, I don't know how he worked on it without our seeing it. Like other girls my age, I have a "Betsy-Wetsy" doll that is my "baby." It will be some 30 years before the introduction of Barbie. Sometimes I wonder how it is that little girls have gone from pretending to be Mommies to preparing to be beauty queens.

In the spring, there are lilacs blooming in our big back yard, the heady smell surrounding my sister and me on days when it's warm enough for us to be down on all fours, playing Jacks or marbles. Being five years younger than her, I like making little creatures and bowls of 'food' out of the patch of red clay in the ground near our house. The clay is cool and smooth, unlike the gritty dirt that sticks to my legs. I sit happily making up stories for a long time -- Mommy is making supper and she's having soup -- I pour water from a dented old measuring cup into one of the clay bowls. And she bakes potatoes -- little oval clay pellets go on a platter. And there's lemonade -- --

One day, before I'm old enough to go to the movies, my mother hands me a cherry lollipop and sends me out to play in the garden. She tells me not to run with the lollipop in my mouth. I clatter through the screen-door and there before me is the long path through the yellow cosmos taller than I am, the leaning purple pansies I think have faces, and the pink and white four-o'clocks buzzing with bees. By the back fence, our calico mama cat rubs against a post warmed by the sun. I take off down the wooden steps and sail down the path, flying like a bird, lollipop firmly tucked in my jaw. I do not trip.

My mother is by my side in an instant. She grabs me by the arm and throws my lollipop into a corner of the yard. "Didn't I just tell you not to run with the lollipop on your mouth? You could fall and choke to death!" She's angry, but I am angrier; my cherry lollipop is over there in the dirt. "Gawdammit!" I shriek. Snatching me up, she carries me into the house, sits me down hard on the kitchen sink drain-board, and lathers a washcloth with Ivory soap. She washes my mouth out with it, and keeps me inside the rest of the day.

I still recall how indignant I felt. Couldn't she see I was flying?

On rainy days I ride my red tricycle madly up and down the long inside hall. In the early Pittsburgh winters when it seems to snow every week, I go sled-riding with my sister on Pierpont Street, just a couple of blocks away. When we move away from Bigham Street to an apartment, I am old enough to have ball-bearing roller skates that clamp onto the soles of my shoes, and we spend long hours out on the sidewalk.

And even though I love sitting curled up with a book most days after school, I find I'm enjoying gym classes more than I used to. By third grade, I begin to win races. When we have standing broad-jump competitions, my long legs outdistance many of the other girls. It's a great feeling, knowing my body will do what I want it to do.

My sister is dreamy and quiet a lot of the time. She sits for hours sketching pictures with soft-leaded #2 pencils in big scrapbooks. As a small child, I often feel that we don't know each other very well - - she was in school by the time I was born. Tall and thin, my sister is blue-eyed like my mother but with straight, honey-colored hair. When I am four or so, she's always being asked to look after me and gets good and tired of it. Her preteen friends think I am a baby. She brings every childhood disease home from school and by the time I come down with it too, she's feeling better. Then she tells me jokes and reads me stories. I don't remember my mother ever telling me a story.

My sister likes to spend more time with me when I get old enough for her to teach me to read. We sit on the front porch, or half-way up the steps leading to the second floor, where she points to letters while we sing the A-B-C song. Then she carefully pronounces words in easy library books, and I say them after her. I proudly get my own library card when I am five. Because of her patience, I am already a reader before my first day of school. Though we grow apart in later years, I will always remember that it was she who gave me the key to another universe.

Between 1940 and 1947, my family moves three times from one corner of Mount Washington to the other, first to a small second floor apartment across the street from a saloon, with a hallway impossible to heat in winter (no one ever wants to go to the bathroom). Late in 1943, we rent the Southern Avenue house. My mother loves this place with its elegant entranceway, French doors by the dining area, and an honest-to-goodness furnace in the basement. We all hope we can settle there for good.

On a humid Saturday in 1945, I am standing at the kitchen sink washing up the lunch dishes. I turn over in my mind the changes that the year has brought. It's hard when there are too many changes at once--especially, big changes. Just this April, President Roosevelt died. He's the only president I've ever known. Franklin Delano Roosevelt had become president in March, 1933. I was born in August of that year. As young children, my sister and I hear endless discussions -- and lots of arguments -- between our Republican father and Democrat mother about FDR and his programs. Like a second language, we absorb the jargon of the times: The Great Depression, unemployment, breadlines, relief, WPA. One of the big things we learn from our mother is that FDR's policies helped put food on our table and keep our family afloat during the tough Depression years. He's always been a hero to me. The whole family gathers around our Philco radio when he broadcasts his Fireside Chats. Like our solid old dining table, he's been planted firmly in the middle of everything important that is going on around me. What will we do without him?

And then in early August, we get some wonderful news: My parents tell my sister and me that they've finally saved up enough money to buy this house. We're thrilled that we won't have to keep moving around.

We all gather round the evening my father calls the landlord, but the smile disappears from his face as he listens. There's a stunned look now as he mumbles something, and hangs up the phone. Shoulders sagging, he takes off his glasses and rubs his eyes as if to see better. It doesn't help. Finally, he gives us what we know will be bad news: "He's promised the house to his son-in-law just back from the war, as soon as our lease is up."

This house will never be ours. We'll have to move again in a few months. My mother lets out a little whimper. Her face goes white and she runs upstairs. My father's body is hunched as though expecting another blow. He steps out back to have a cigarette. Stunned and sad, my sister and I just look at each other—we had come so close. We knew how much our parents had given up to be able to afford this house. They'd sold the car. They even decided to let go of the little wooden cabin my father had built with his own hands, in Imperial, Pennsylvania. During the hottest part of the last few summers, we'd spent a week or two there, loving the country feel of it. All of that was gone, and this would be our third move in seven years. When would we ever be able to put down roots?

Change. It seems like the one sure thing. In just a couple of years, I'll be starting Senior High. I'm growing up. What will the new school be like? I stare out at the garden, slowly lulled away from my thoughts by its late-summer beauty. Warm rinse water bathes my hands as I watch a Monarch butterfly float outside the window.

The sound of a phone receiver slammed back into its cradle startles me. I turn around and there, through the open doorway, I see my father standing with his hands around my mother's neck.

I turn icy cold. They see me looking at them and for a second, no one moves. I don't really know what to do. What if I make things worse? My mind insists this can't be happening. The sun is streaming through the French doors, making fluid squares on the polished floor. All is quiet except for the water left running in the kitchen. Then I remember: it's payday. My father's had too much to drink.

"Take your hands off her!"

I rush forward to push him away but stop before I reach them. Something has changed. For a fleeting moment, I see anguish in his eyes, and then he looks away. His hands drop to his sides. "Di'nt mean nothin'—don't need to call the cops on me."

He walks carefully into the living room, as if the floor were tilted. I take a deep breath and thank God my father hadn't passed the danger point. What if he hadn't backed down? Still charged with adrenalin, my whole body is shaking.

I turn to look at my mother. She forces a little smile and says "It's all right. He came home looking for a fight and started to get a little rough. I threatened to call the police." My mother seems calm; she's had to handle him before. I wonder how many times this scene played out in the past, when no one else was home?

My mother's a strong-minded woman. I think the only time he feels he can stand up to her is when he's had a few too many beers. In between these times, he must be tamping down his frustration at losing his family, trying to swallow his anger at my mother's obstinacy and maybe his own bad decisions. Shortly after this, my sister looks in my mother's diary one day. She finds a page where it says: "My husband hit me again today." I think my sister already suspected what was going on, but the day I surprised him with his hands on her neck was my first realization that he might actually hurt her. The diary proved he already had.

For a long while afterwards, I struggle with a sense of out-of-control-ness. What will I do if it happens again? What if the alcohol working on his brain stops him from feeling anything but the anger? This crisis is over, but I still worry about the tension that underlies our family life. My thoughts return to 1943, when we were expecting unusual visitors: two of my father's grown children from his first marriage.

Before their arrival, my mother puts eggs on to boil for the salad, and hurries out to the store for something she's forgotten. The eggs boil dry and explode, leaving pieces stuck to the ceiling. The pot is blackened, smoking. The pungent odor of burnt food drifts slowly from the kitchen into the living room.

When she returns, Daniel and Fannie are already sitting on the sofa. Both are in their early twenties; she's sweet-faced, a little on the plump side, he's dark-eyed and handsome, with the rugged good looks my father had when he was younger. They've arrived sooner than expected, and are looking a little uncomfortable as my teenage sister struggles to make conversation. My father is nowhere in sight.

Red-faced, my mother apologizes for the smell and the mess in the kitchen; there is no time to clean up. I notice that she seems to have as much trouble talking to them as my sister does. Nervously, she calls upstairs to my father and getting no answer, goes up to check. Seeing that the bathroom door is closed, she tells them he must still be shaving.

Why is my father so late coming down? Young as I am, I sense the strain on everyone in the room. All I know at this point is that these two (and a younger brother, Richard, who is a soldier overseas) are my father's children, too, but they've never lived with us. I don't know why.

Finally, we hear his slow footsteps on the stairs. Fanny and Daniel look up curiously. He's cut himself shaving and a little thread of blood shows on his chin. What we can't help noticing are his eyes. They're red from crying. My half-brother gets up to shake his hand and talks quickly about their drive up from Kentucky. My mother fades into the kitchen to salvage lunch.

I won't remember the words I hear that day. I know only that my father has visited them a few times while they were growing up.

Most years he couldn't afford to do that. When he did, he would come back looking tired and sad. He talked little. How must he have felt having three other growing children that he never saw in a school play, or pitching an exciting game? I imagine he'd mourned the fact that when they came home feeling rotten -- or really happy -- he wouldn't be there to listen. There in the living room, surrounded by four of his five children, my father is forced to realize that his first family has grown up without knowing his financial support, without his presence, and probably not suspecting the depth of his regret. It's obvious that there aren't any shared experiences we can all laugh about. Nobody plans any get-togethers. My father doesn't even bring out the photo albums – I guess, because his firstborn children aren't in them. Eventually my mother comes in with trays of food. It helps to have something to do with our hands.

Now, I sit recalling the strained faces of my older siblings. It seems to me their unspoken feelings might have been like an indigestible meal they'd already eaten. They sat there, politely swallowing their ham sandwiches on top of it.

My father never seemed to me like the kind of man who would deliberately abandon his family. When my mother stuck to her original decision not to raise his first three children, he couldn't see any way out of his predicament. Divorce was not the convenient answer then that it is now. Not only were women seldom prepared to take on the bread-winning role in the family, but there was much more social stigma attached for both the husband and wife who ended a marriage.

As I am writing this memoir, my half sister-in-law, now widowed, sends me information that shows my father and his younger sister, Cece, had been abandoned by *their* father when he was three years old. His mother's second husband, a gambling man nicknamed Smitty, also walked away from the family. This explains so much. My father had himself been abandoned *twice* before he was six years old. I learn this sad truth only now, when I am in my seventies. It would have helped me to understand and forgive him.

When my father switches from his regular four to midnight shift to working nights at the gas plant, we, his second family, don't see much of him because he sleeps in the daytime. Maybe that's why my parents don't argue so much anymore. Or maybe it's just that this is an old fight, and they are tired of fighting it.

My father hardly ever misses work. He is a good provider. But as the years go by, our family grows to hate paydays.

On these days, the days most families look forward to, when their fathers buy treats and pay off bills, a man who is no longer my father staggers into the house, slack-jawed and befuddled. His speech is slurred. My sister and I hate the way he sounds and smells when he's been drinking. We are silent and don't want to look at him. That makes him angry. He rocks back and forth on his feet and narrows his eyes at us. "Wassamatter? You can't say hello to your father? What'd I do, huh? Did I do sumthin' to you?" We still don't answer. What is there to say? "Too many damn women in this house for me, thass what." Our mother tries to get him to sit down and eat. Sometimes she's kept dinner waiting for more than an hour. She's tense and out of sorts. By this time none of us is hungry.

In the spring of 1946, we move one last time: we buy a 'handyman special' on Gaskell Street. My father is thrilled because he loves this kind of work: replacing patches of old rotted wood with hardy new pieces of lumber; cutting to fit and laying fresh linoleum in the kitchen; spackling and painting the bathroom. He painstakingly covers the wooden house with Inselbric, an insulated waterproof exterior popular in the forties because the homeowner can forget about yearly house-painting. Maybe best of all, he persuades the man who sells us the house to throw in the empty lot next door. It's all choked with weeds so the man is glad to get rid of it for a little extra. Together we rip out the tall, tough overgrowth, dig up stumps and stones, and cut back the ragged hedges that border the front.

Magically, over the summer months, we create a green oasis. A wide swath of lawn stretches upward from the hedges to where Seven

Sister roses bloom, just behind the red and white glider swing. My father's vegetable garden thrives in the upper yard with corn, tomatoes, snap beans, rhubarb, and lettuce. On the side where the slate steps curve down near our back door, my mother creates a rock garden with peat moss, alyssum, and Sweet William. For a little while, at least, I think all of us are happier than we have ever been.

Sinew

The year before we discover my scoliosis, I am thirteen and just beginning eighth grade. The first week, I learn to my horror that swimming is mandatory. Some of my classmates love the idea, but it makes me sick to my stomach. I've been afraid of the water since I waded into a six-inch creek to watch minnows when I was five years old. I stepped on a sharp rock, and felt myself falling into the cold water, sure on the way down I was going to drown. My sister hauled me out, but that early stab of panic is still with me.

On swim days, I start feeling tense at breakfast; it gets worse on the way to school, and by the time I put on the regulation gray knit swim suit that emphasizes my boniness, I just want the double period to be over. But I do what I hate because no student can pass the grade with a failing mark in swimming. Very slowly, with help from two good swimmers, I learn to float and then do the crawl stroke in four feet of water, even though my legs tend to sink because I don't have a strong kick. This takes most of the first year, but my fear recedes as my skill increases.

One day the locker room chatter seems more apprehensive than usual; there is a rumor we will be asked to do something new. Good. For once, nearly everyone is as nervous as I am. We hop in and out of the icy foot disinfectant in the doorway leading to the pool, adjusting slowly to breathing the chlorine-bathed humidity trapped in this vast space.

After a brief warm-up -- jumping up and down at the four-foot end of the pool – we're told that everyone who can do the crawl will be asked to dive from the board at the deep end of the pool. Suddenly subdued, our class of 20-odd girls lines up and one by one, dives off the board into eight feet of aqua green water. We are instructed to turn underwater and push up from the bottom till we break the surface.

Fine. I can do this, I think.

I'm still fearful, but am beginning to feel, too, the exciting sense of being challenged and wanting to meet that challenge. As each girl before me has her turn, the class erupts into squeals at the belly-smackers and cheers for the three or four girls who cut the water cleanly.

It is my turn. Readying myself, I remember to tuck my head down between my outstretched arms and enter the water well. Once below the surface, my momentary elation is gone. I'm not far enough up to reach the surface, not far enough down to push with my feet on the bottom. Flailing, I choke on swallowed water. Then my eyes focus on the end of a long bamboo pole just in front of me—the pole I know Miss O'Toole uses to fish people in trouble out of the water.

Taking great gulps of air, wanting to spit out the taste of chlorine, I crawl out and sit shivering under a big towel, aware of sympathetic glances from friends. O'Toole, still frowning with displeasure, returns to the diving tryouts. For several long minutes, I berate myself. Then I decide I am going to learn to swim well and pass the Red Cross test in ninth grade.

When summer comes, I go to a neighborhood pool in the mornings when it's not crowded, and practice the required strokes, doing pool-widths in the four-foot section. I'm enjoying the smooth slap of the water and the sensual feeling of sliding through it. No instructor, no noisy class, just me and the water, working together. The awful tension is gone, and in its place is something close to confidence.

In September, I'm ready to practice length-wise laps of the pool and discover that there are free-swim periods some days after school. There are only eight of us; most of the others are preparing for the test, like me. Red Cross requirements are to swim a total of five lengthwise laps, consecutively, three of them in crawl stroke and the remaining two in side, breast, or back stroke. This can be done in any order. We also must perform a simulated rescue by cupping our hand under a buddy's chin and side-stroking to a designated point.

The hardest thing for me now is getting used to swimming pool lengths instead of widths. I get short of breath and need to stop in between laps. I won't be able to do this in the actual test. When I think how far I've come in the last year I know I can't stop now; I'm almost there. With a few more weeks of after-school practice, my breathing capacity improves. The test is now two weeks off.

I enjoy these small after-school sessions, but during regular school hours, there is a double swim period twice a week. There are many more kids that I know in the regular classes, which makes for complications. It's now several months since I saw the doctor about my back. When I undress, I must get in and out of the brace I wear beneath my clothes. At the beginning of every swim period, I disappear into one of the booths in the adjoining ladies' room, undress, wrap the brace in a towel, come out and throw it in my locker. Then, usually a little late, I head for the pool. After class, I do the whole thing in reverse. It takes me at least four or five minutes in the booth each time, while the other girls undress and dress by their lockers. I can't bring myself to tell anyone why I'm doing this, and the idea of hooking and buckling my brace in front of everyone is out of the question.

One swim class day, as I frantically remove my clothes in the stall, I hear some of the girls just outside speculating on my secret activities in the 'john.' Marilyn Standish, the best swimmer in the class, rivets everyone's attention. "That Rosalyn! What on earth does she do in there all the time?" Another girl yells, "Hey, hurry up, I have to pee before I hit that cold water!" And then, there are whispers I can barely make out. I catch one sentence: "Do you think she's playing with herself?" I groan inwardly.

That night I tell my mother how long it takes to change, how I'm always late for my next class, and that I can't stand the situation much longer. I don't tell her what the girls are saying.

Two weeks later, I slip into the water, knowing that I am ready. I do two laps of crawl, one back stroke to rest a bit, then another crawl, and end with a side stroke, which is my favorite. I perform the rescue procedure without a hitch. Clutching the card that says I've passed, every part of me is limp with joy and relief. Not only have I performed well, my mother has talked with someone at the school. From now on, I'm excused from swimming. I take attendance the rest of the year and keep my clothes on. Still, it feels funny to be sitting on a poolside bleacher with a couple of girls who have heart murmurs when I know I can swim well enough to save someone's life.

For months before this, I barely get to algebra class before the bell rings because it takes so long to dry my long hair after swimming. Flustered and out of breath, I feel behind anyway; when it comes to finding 'X,' I have serious doubts about my intelligence. One day, while the class is working out word problems, Miss Anderson beckons me into the hall. Uh-oh, she's going to fuss about my constant lateness.

But Miss Anderson, who's also our student counselor and special events coordinator, asks a question that sends a warm wave of relief cascading through me: "I wonder if you'd like to give me a hand with some clerical help – in my office, during algebra class? There are things I'm not getting to, and it would be such a help!" I quickly agree, and she adds, "Don't worry about your grade. I'll tutor you so you will pass algebra."

One day, instead of having me file student records, Miss Anderson says she needs a poster to advertise a school play she's producing. I take some materials home and come back the next day with the poster. It feels fantastic. I'd never realized that someone like me could create something useful to a school; schools have always been about adults and authority. Later on, Miss Anderson arranges for me to spend some study periods with her, where I produce more posters and design a few props for plays. Sometimes she asks what I think I might like to do after graduation. That seems far away, so I put her off.

But then I go home with the question buzzing in my head. That leads to more questions—what do I really love doing—so much so that I wouldn't mind doing it every day? The answer has to be writing or artwork. And since I became a teenager, I've become fascinated with fashion. I've been reading every word of Kaufmann's full-page newspaper ads, studying the department store's fashion layout and copy as if it were required homework. The next time Miss Anderson asks about my post-graduation plans, I confide that I'd like to write advertising copy. She encourages me to keep improving my writing and artistic abilities to ready myself for an ad job. Over these months, I feel a gathering excitement, a reinforcement of possibility. I don't have to wait for something to happen and react; I can prepare myself to make something happen.

In the fall of 1948, I enter a much larger Senior High School which draws students from several surrounding districts. I walk to school in a state of high excitement, looking forward to seeing my friends again. The first period in home room I keep waiting for one to walk in, but none of them show up. Moving through the day, it becomes clear that I will have no classes with any of the kids I feel most comfortable with; I don't even run into them in the hallway. I must start all over again.

It's hard not to feel lost in the swirl of hundreds of students in the halls. No one knows that I write poetry and love to dance. That I made props for Junior High plays and covered basketball games for the school newspaper. Does anyone care if I'm alive?

I catch a few people glancing at the weird ridges underneath my sweater, then looking away. Anger pokes up beneath my loneliness. I used to have friends who didn't even see my brace. They would tease me about wanting to cover the guys' intramural basketball games because I liked Louie, the star player. The boys and I would jitterbug at school dances to the jazzy sounds of Benny Goodman. Working to put out the school newspaper, we were a team that learned from and respected one another. Being with them helped me forget I even wore the brace. Over the summer, I lost touch with them because their families vacationed out of town. Now I wonder whether they're on another schedule or if they've moved away. Why can't things be the same as they used to be?

I grow self-conscious again. I hate the brace but still need to wear it. How can I have forgotten that I'm different, and always will be? In this state of mind, it's months before things begin to change – and then, I make two friends inside of a week.

In Miss Ellis's eleventh grade English class, our assignment is to read *A Tale of Two Cities*, and then tell part of the story from the point of view of one of its characters. I pore over parts of the narrative again that evening, and then sit staring at our cat. She's carefully washing her paw and looking oblivious, though I know she knows I'm watching her. Suddenly, I don't want to write this piece from the viewpoint of any of the major characters. I want to create something different. I'll have my narrator be the guillotine itself. And she's a woman, Madame La Guillotine, not only a witness to the horrendous events of that time, but a character who plays a crucial role in the story. The guillotine describes the vengeful Madame DeFarge – a secret revolutionary – as she sits on the porch of her wine-shop, the stitches in her knitting recording the names of those who must die. Because DeFarge herself has suffered at the hands of the oppressive Evremonde family, she feels only hate toward Charles Darnay who is a blood-relation of that family, and Lucie Manette, related to it by marriage. Charles and Lucie love each other. They are moral human beings and haven't been part of this history of oppression. DeFarge sees them as aristocrats and wants them dead. La Guillotine is not sentimental; she revels in the role of final judge and jury, and seeing to it that those marked guilty don't escape. She welcomes Sidney Carton to her dread platform – the brilliant but aimless alcoholic who loves Lucie as well – not realizing she'll be cheated of the other two because Carton's sacrificial decision goads him to die so that Charles and Lucie can be together.

The day I am called on to present my story, I go to the front, nervously clearing my throat. Holding my composition in one hand, I furiously twist my pen with the other, behind my back. Very aware of Miss Ellis, who sits at her desk to my right, I begin. Somewhere around the third paragraph, I look up and notice the class has stopped whispering and shuffling. They are completely quiet. What I've written is making them see me in a different way.

After class, Nita McCaffrey looks over at me and circles her thumb and finger in an "OK" sign. I have noticed this freckle-faced girl with reddish hair, who sits behind me on my left. So many girls answer teachers' questions with a coy air, not thinking about their answer but about the boys who are watching. She's not like that. I smile at her now and tell her how frightened I was. She laughs and says, "But it didn't keep you from writing a great paper, did it? Why don't you join us on the Spectator newspaper club? We need people like you!"

After school a couple of days later, I walk into the messy room where the newspaper is put together and feel at home: there are the mimeograph machine, the stacks of paper, the boxes of stencils and styluses – all the tools I learned to use back in the fifth grade. Nita introduces me, and as she does so, I see that Miss Ellis is sitting at a table on the side; I hadn't realized she was the faculty advisor for the Spectator. But now she isn't wearing the stern face I see in the classroom. She's smiling.

Nita walks home the same way I do, and so does her friend, Linda Beale. Linda is blue-eyed with hair the color of hay. Her pale slenderness contrasts with Nita's mature body and ruddy complexion. My skinny frame and curly brown hair add yet another contrast. We are a variegated threesome. It's so good to have friends again.

My sister writes from California with unexpected news: she's coming home. She'd been living and working there for more than two years, when one morning she woke to find her room mate gone, along with her radio, camera, and cash on hand. Ashamed to tell us what happened, she somehow managed for a little while, and then was laid off from her job. My folks are upset; they had hoped she would be independent by now. Reluctantly, they wire her money they don't really have for the return trip.

Now she brings her suitcase upstairs and sits on the twin bed opposite mine, just where it's always been. She looks wonderingly at the room around her, arranged much as when she left, but its whole aspect changed by the turquoise plaid wallpaper I've chosen to replace the pink rosebuds she remembers.

"I was really upset when I looked in the drawer for my money and there was nothing left. Then I saw that the other things had disappeared, too. I didn't start to cry until it hit me that Donna had only been pretending to be my friend."

Listening to her story, it occurs to me that, once I got over the shock of having scoliosis, I've actually been pretty happy the last couple of years. Her life was supposed to take off when she left for California. Instead, through no fault of her own, it has reversed.

My sister was often the capable, responsible big sister who explained puzzling things like menstruation and what "homosexual" meant. But I do recall she began to have life puzzles of her own that no one could help her solve. By her early teens she spent long hours listening to popular music instead of doing her homework. She propped movie magazines inside her English textbook in class and got caught doing it. She said her English teacher 'had it in' for her. Finally, she flunked eleventh grade and never went back.

Later on, my sister seemed to settle down. She spent months in a practical nursing course. Every class day, she came home all excited, reporting on what she was learning. But when graduation time rolled around, her supervisor refused to certify her; saying she was 'too nervous' to do this kind of work. My sister thought maybe her hand was shaking during the test when they practiced bandaging and tourniquets, under the teacher's critical eye. My heart ached for her. We knew she was highly motivated and had studied hard in that class; failing to get the certification was a crushing blow.

Did she act up and do poorly in her earlier life for the same reason I tried to be good and please everyone? We both craved attention. Then when she actually buckled down and worked hard at learning something that would get her a decent job, why didn't it work for her? My sister kept hitting brick walls: She'd wanted to develop her artistic talent and had once thought she might be able to go to a specialized art school, but that turned out to be too expensive. She was told by her high school art teacher that she shouldn't bother trying to succeed as an artist; she wasn't good enough. We were two hungry people. Somehow, I eventually managed to find support and encouragement outside our family; she had trouble doing that.

When I turn sixteen, my mother says I can go with my sister to a downtown roller-skating rink where they have bouncy, live organ music and people who help you learn the skate-dance steps. She has a lot of fun there, and wants me to go too. Both of us are already seasoned roller skaters, from years ago when we negotiated the gravelly sidewalks and uneven bricks of Shiloh Street. The first time I show up at the rink, I'm awestruck at the huge skating arena set beneath cavernous rafters. The high old windows look as if they haven't been opened for years. But the action down below is what fills the place with excitement. It takes a while to get used to the speed at which the skaters travel. Gathering my courage, I stand with my skates on, sipping a cherry coke over at the corner snack bar. Watching the organist jive on his bench in the glassed-in balcony, I feel the music inviting my body to move. I want to be out there – but what if I fall?

I let my sister and her friend pull me out on the floor – and I'm doing it! Pennsylvania Polka, My Happiness, Five Minutes More. In the first twenty minutes, they teach me how to two-step (the easiest) and I'm dancing along, just like everybody else. Wow. I'm flying again. I relax, relying on the smooth coordination I'd had as a child.

During breaks, I watch the couples gracefully turning into waltz steps on the slower numbers. I'll never have the courage to turn in mid-stride, and skate backwards. So I don't try to waltz, but I don't dwell on falling either.

The rink is where I meet my first love at seventeen. Stephen is tall and rangy, with a lopsided grin. He's eight years older, which makes the relationship all the more exciting. It's great fun going to movies and on picnics with him -- the whole dating experience I haven't had up till now. We join the crowd at outdoor summer concerts in Schenley Park, where part of the magic is dusk falling softly around us as we listen to Gershwin and Romberg. He likes to do all kinds of things, and has enough money to occasionally take me where I might not otherwise get to go. One special evening we hear Louis Armstrong at Syria Mosque. He is the first black person I have ever seen perform in person. The evening vibrates as the great warmth of his personality and power of his trumpet-playing reach out to wrap everyone in a web of love and possibility. Finally, mopping his face with a huge white handkerchief, he invites us all to join him in the finale. He swings into a rousing, foot-stomping rendition of "When the Saints Go Marching In," cheeks bulging, trumpet pointed to the sky. Everyone is on their feet, clapping and singing, hoping to catch some of his spirit to take home with them.

Stephen is fun to spend time with, and important to me in a wholly other way. He's the first man who kisses me, makes me feel like a woman. Sometimes he surprises me when I'm fixing something in the kitchen, and wraps his arms around me from behind. If he's aware that my back feels different, he doesn't mention it. And I'm experiencing my body as a vessel of pleasure for the first time in my adult life. As the months go by, I long to do whatever it is that people do when they feel this urging. In 1950, I know absolutely nothing about sex, and neither does my sister. The dictionary is no help because I don't know what words to search for. I scour Walt Whitman's Leaves of Grass, turned on by its ebullient evocation of the erotic, but alas, it's not written to educate young girls about sexual exploration. What does make an impression on me is that my sister has a friend who, right around that time, "went too far and got in trouble." She has a baby. Another mystery-- but it serves to check my thirst for adventure in this area. During the two years we go together, Stephen and I show our affection by kissing and holding each other, but never go beyond that.

All this time, I daydream that in the distant future we might be married. But when he begins to urge me to marry soon, I worry that what I feel for him is more an adolescent crush than a mature love. One morning at breakfast, my mother looks me in the eye and says, "Rosalyn, I can see you and Stephen are serious. If you want to get married, it's okay with us. We'll buy you something you'll need, maybe a stove or refrigerator. You two talk it over and let us know what you decide."

I sit, unbelieving, in my room, knowing that things are falling apart, and it's my own fault. My parents have given their blessing to a relationship I haven't been honest about with myself -- or with Stephen. My mother's offer makes me confront the truth: I've loved being with Stephen and entertaining the distant romantic dream of marriage. But I'm far from ready to marry anyone. I'm not sure if I even love him. Maybe I'm just in love with the idea of being loved.

Over the next few days, I make the anguished decision to break up with him. It's a decision filled with loss and longing. I have found someone who loves me and anticipates marriage. I care for him. I've even pictured how our children might look. Am I throwing away a chance at happiness? I know I don't love him enough to spend a lifetime with him. How will I ever tell him that?

He reaches out, enveloping me in a hug. Neither of us speaks for a long time. He is having a hard time with it, as I am. He seems searching for words, but says nothing as we draw apart. "I haven't learned much about what love looks like in my house," I said. "You helped me know what it is like to be loved. Thank you for that." His voice comes out like a half-sob, "Then why can't we continue?" I tell him I need a lot more time to figure myself out. "The time to do that is before I think of settling down. I want to know who I am before I get married."

Walking back from the park, he takes my hand. "I understand how you feel, but let's give it a little time and meet again, okay?" I agree. Maybe winding down slowly might help us to heal the hurt.

I feel empty after we talk, but yet in some deeper place, relieved. Besides explaining my feelings to him, I've had to face the unexamined reasons why I stayed with him so long: I was barely seventeen when we first met, and flattered by the attention of an older man. I was eager for the experience of real "dates," which I'd never had before. It was great going out two or three times a week, and finally having a fellow to tell my girlfriends about. My confidence had soared. I was normal.

The next time we meet, he is standing beside the new car he's bought. I'm not sure if this is to remind me how well he's doing, or if it's his consolation prize. As we ride around, he says it's natural that at nineteen, I might have the jitters about getting married. This doesn't change my mind; I still trust my intuition. Our conversation goes off, circles around, comes back to what we said before. We see each other a few more times, then, let it go.

Right decision or not, the pain of suddenly not being together hangs on. My mother gets tired of my moping around the house. She shows me an item in the paper about the Young Men's Christian

Association (YMCA), where they have a choir, workshops, and weekly dances. Sounds kind of interesting, I think with a sigh. But it means starting over. Life is all about endings, and starting over.

On a Thursday night in the spring of 1953, I walk into the "Y" on Wood Street and follow the music. It feels like I'm back in the high school gym —the lineup of young women sitting on one side of the long room -- bored, annoyed, hopeful, despairing. The blur of couples whirling by: the lucky chosen. I love that the lighting is low; the big band sound large and loud. When a partner appears, my feet know what to do, and I relax. I'm going to enjoy coming here to dance.

One evening, as I take time out to rest, I find myself smiling. I enjoy listening to the music almost as much as dancing. A tall, slender man bends toward me, looking nervous. His face creases in a smile when I get up to dance. As we move slowly around the darkened room, I think that he's not as good a dancer as some of the men I've met there. But there's something about him…what is it…that I like a lot. He isn't smooth. He doesn't have a "line."

What a wonderful relief.

In between dance sets, we keep talking. I tell him about writing ad copy for Pittsburgh Mercantile department store on the city's South Side. "The job started off a little bumpy—no on ever asked me if I could type. They were aghast when I turned in my first copy-- handwritten." David chuckles as I tell the rest. "Lucky we had an old Underwood at home. I had to teach myself how to type over the weekend."

David is studying evenings for a master's degree in psychology at Pitt. He's a Commissions Clerk at Penn Mutual Life Insurance Company, and has his own funny work story: "Each of the employees' phones has a different ring, and after hours, just for the heck of it, some of them 'play the switch-board.'" Laughing, we drift back out on the floor.

"There's this huge window right by my desk," I tell him. "Today I kept staring out at the big J&L steel mill across the street. I'd never seen it like that before. There were brilliant red-orange flames coming out of the tall stacks, and the sky behind them was this deep, charcoal gray—it took my breath away. I couldn't keep my mind on my work until I'd written a poem about it."

"You'll have to show it to me -- I'd like to read it. I don't write poetry, but I do write music."

Funny, I've never once mentioned writing poetry to a man before. And no one I've danced with ever said he wrote music. We match our steps to the sweet sax solo behind us, and I feel my spirits rising.

Ah, yes, a new beginning. I like this man.

Though we enjoy seeing each other at the dances, we don't start dating for a long time. Over the next year there is an emotional war going on inside me. I turn twenty in the summer of 1953, and part of me longs for a closer relationship. The other voice reminds me how much it hurts to break up. So I go to the "Y" on Thursday evenings and dance with lonely men who need companionship and validation as much as I do. I briefly date a couple of them. And I still pay attention to the really smooth dancers.

As David and I get to know each other better, we find that both our fathers have worked at utilities for years. I complain to him about my father's drinking. He mentions having problems with his mother. We even both work for companies called "P.M." for short. Slowly we build an intangible bond of friendship, the kind of comfortable togetherness I didn't know was possible to have with a man.

One afternoon in early 1954, I am sitting in the "Y" coffee shop when David comes through the door. Calling him over, I ask him if he's heard about the bus trip to Estes Park, Colorado, that the "Y" is planning for that summer. He sits down and orders a cold drink. "I did hear something, but wasn't paying much attention." A sudden inspiration makes me bold. "Why don't you come with me? It'll be more fun if we go together!" He is tickled that I asked him. We sip our sodas and plan on seeing each other later that week. After dancing with each other for a year, David and I finally begin to spend more time together.

The Colorado trip turns out to be the most emotionally freeing experience I've ever had. Here we are – friends who are fast developing more than friendly feelings for each other, sitting close to each other for two days and two nights each way on a Greyhound bus. We set off singing "I Am a Happy Wanderer" and "Tell Me Why." Gradually our exuberance segues into a long, dark night a world away from home and admonitions. We share comfortable silences, find ourselves looking long into each other's eyes. Touch each other and love the way it makes us feel.

At Estes Park, though we stay in separate ʼguysʼ and ʼgirlsʼ cabins, by day we're a couple. We walk out in the morning, breathing fresher air than we ever knew in Pittsburgh. We delight in the marbled spread of sky unspoiled by skyscrapers. The comforting presence of the Rocky Mountains enfolds us, and one day a group of us climbs a foothill called Bible Point. Choir practice here is almost a spiritual experience: Men and women who've never sung with each other before gather early on the porch of the central meeting space. The sun sifts in gentle rays through tall trees, lighting our music. We raise our voices as if that were the main reason we had come. There is something magical about Ralph Vaughn Williams accompanied by birdsong at 7:30 A.M.

David and I talk about everything and listen intently. It's almost as though I'm taking notes in my heart, wanting to remember everything because this relationship promises to mean so much more than the last one. These precious days we're able to step away from who we've been at home. We're no longer our parents' children but distinct persons with ideas and opinions of our own. Even the jobs we hold grow distant as we imagine something better. And for me, there is a delicious sense of freedom from old worries about ugliness and limitation. The gargoyles are far away.

At the closing ceremony of the conference, the YMCA announces it will hold a huge international Centennial the following year in Paris. It is scheduled for August, 1955. We exchange wistful glances, but neither of us has enough money to even think about it.

On the long, quiet bus ride home, we talk about change, not only in our own lives but in the world around us. We've been reading about the 'Jim Crow' laws in the south that created separate public accommodations like waiting rooms and drinking fountains labeled "Whites Only" and "Coloreds Only." It's obvious that black children's education there is certainly inferior to the education white children receive. We'd welcomed the Supreme Court decision, Brown v. Board of Education, handed down that spring (1954), which outlawed racial segregation in public schools. It's hard for us to understand the extreme racial divisiveness in the south, yet we've grown up in all white neighborhoods and won't realize until much later how racial steering by politicians and realtors has been at work in our northern communities for decades. We've stopped asking why we don't encounter black people in our everyday lives. When we asked that question as children, people would cut us off quickly with: "They prefer to live with their own kind" or "When they move into a neighborhood, the property values go down." While David and I travel home on the bus, discussing the new law we hope will change things in the South, August Wilson is growing up in the all-black Hill District of Pittsburgh -- only a few miles away from where we live. He's coming up hard, but learning how to use his familiarity with the distance between black and white to eventually write plays like *The Piano Lesson* and *Two Trains Running*. Much later, when we see his work, we'll realize again how much richer our lives would have been if we could have gotten to know these folks.

When I was eleven, I brought home a new friend that had just started to my school. Her name was Lily, and we had a great time talking on the way over to my house. My mother smiled at her, set out milk and cookies while we did our homework together at the big grey Formica kitchen table. I walked Lily to the trolley stop a couple of hours later, thinking how much fun we were going to have together.

The next morning, my mother was unusually quiet. Then, she turned from the stove and told me that I couldn't be Lily's friend. In the middle of eating my cereal, I looked up in disbelief. "What? But...but you liked her, I could tell." "She may be a nice little girl, but you know your father won't like it if you bring her here again. It will just cause trouble– she's a Negro."

I felt a tearing at my insides. In our home, we kids never talked back to our parents. I had never wanted to before. But how could I make her see how wrong this was? "I know that she's a Negro. It doesn't make any difference to me. I like being with her."

"Rosalyn, I've already talked with your father about this. I don't want to hear any arguments. You must tell her today in school that you can't be her friend. And don't bring her back again."

Hot rage boiled up, but I knew there was nothing I could say that would change anything. When she mentioned my father, it was clear to me that no argument would help. She may have even argued with him on my side, but he was the head of the family and she wanted to keep the peace. Helpless and seething, I got up quickly, leaving my cereal half eaten, and ran upstairs to vent my frustration. Ten minutes later, I left for school, red-eyed and miserable.

When I saw Lily that day, all the joy I had felt at knowing her was gone. It was as if I'd had stones for breakfast. She saw the stricken look on my face, her grin fading. "My parents say I can't be your friend. It's not me, it's them. I'm so sorry—I like you."

There were tears in my eyes, and in hers, at first. Then, as I gazed at her, she blinked and a sort of cool quietness inhabited them. Her voice sounded old as she answered. "I understand. Don't worry about it." I wanted to scream at having to hurt her this way. I was hurting, too. Watching her go, I realized she had probably heard these words before. She was the school janitor's daughter, the only black child in an elementary school with 300 students.

Back in Pittsburgh, I come in early for choir practice at the "Y" one January night. There's a group gathered round the piano where a smiling airman in uniform is banging out fantastic boogie-woogie. I stand there, moving with the music, wishing I'd get a chance to talk with him. Later on at the dance, the stranger and I end up spending the evening together, dancing and talking. I like his easy smile and his interesting way of exploring things. He tells me he's only home for a short while and then must go back to his base in another state. I've looked for David more than once, but don't see him anywhere in the crowd, so when the airman offers to see me home, I accept. I'm not sure why I do this; I'm just enjoying the moment and not really thinking of anything else. The man is a perfect gentleman who says goodnight at my door. But David had been there, and is very hurt by my thoughtlessness. When he attended college in Indiana, most of the women were attracted to men coming back from the war, who seemed so much older and more sophisticated. At the dance, David feels, all over again, that he is competing on an uneven playing field. Though we'd agreed to still sometimes date and dance with others if we wanted to, he questions the closeness of the relationship he thought we had. He is right. What am I doing? It shows me that I haven't completely stopped wanting to explore other relationships. He thought for a while it was the end of ours.

The questions about David persist, even when I try to will them away. We have so much in common – yet there are big differences between us, too.

David already has a college degree and is working toward his Master's. I doubt if I'll ever get to college. My parents were hoping I'd get a scholarship; when I didn't, they told me they couldn't afford to send me to college. Then I learned about a Distributive Education Program I could join in twelfth grade. I liked the idea of spending my mornings on business math and English to earn my diploma, and training to work in a retail store in the afternoons. So, I began working at seventeen, while still in high school. But I never stopped wanting to go to college. When I met David, I started to understand how much more there was to know. I promised myself that someday I was going to make time to explore.

The way we see religion, too, is very different. In the beginning of our relationship, I was glad that we both were members of Protestant churches during our growing-up years, and that we share a passion for social justice. But he confides soon after we meet that he's decided to become a Unitarian. I had never heard of that denomination. A little afraid of what he was going to say, I asked what Unitarians believed.

"That each of us can use our intellect to seek out our own truth; that's what appeals to me. From the time I was eight or nine years old, I read books my uncles had about astronomy, evolution, and how huge the universe really is. I've always admired Jesus' life and work and believed strongly in Christian ethics. But after a while, I began to question accepted Christian theology, especially when I did more reading in college. Why would God send his son to save only us, in the middle of this vast universe? Why would a man like Jesus whose very life taught others how to live, have to be sacrificed? It didn't make sense to me anymore. So now I believe in one God, not a triune God. I see Jesus as a wise guide and teacher, not a deity."

For the naive Bible-believing Christian I am at that time, this speech sets off alarm bells. All my life up to then, I'd heard friends and family warning, "Whatever you do, don't fall in love with someone outside your religion." Now, I'm running smack into that admonition and having to decide whether to acquiesce or resist it with all my might. Am I truly pushing away what I believe in or what I think I believe in? I've gone to the same Methodist church for the last thirteen years, and have been active in the Youth Fellowship. Yet, with all this grounding, there's a maverick side of me that raises objections once in a while: Why do the folks in my church think it's sinful to play cards if you don't gamble? Why do they frown on dancing? (I love to play rummy almost as much as I love to dance).

The year before this, right after I broke up with Stephen, I felt very vulnerable. One evening I took the trolley out to Oakland, where there was a Youth for Christ rally at Syria Mosque. This was the same beautiful old building where I'd gone with Stephen to hear Louis Armstrong. I was excited to see the numbers of teens and young adults arriving and walked inside with them. It's hard to convey the heightened sense I had at that moment that we were entering both sanctuary and crucible, a place where our lives might be changed forever.

The stirring atmosphere of a revival tent spread over us as the choir led the crowd in rousing hymns; the organ continuing softly as we heard the familiar story of Jesus' sacrifice to save us from our sins. "And what are our sins," the minister whispered, almost a voice in our head. "They may be big or little, but we all need to admit we have transgressed. We don't have to shout them out loud, but here—right now—we need to confess their presence, deep in our hearts." Longing was palpable in the room; tears marked the faces of many who had been laughing an hour before. Once more the music surrounded us. "Come, all you who are heavy-laden, come to Jesus, and he will give you rest." As the altar call was given, the choir sang, "Just as I am, without one plea..." It took courage to walk out of one's anonymity. Slowly the first one got up, then more rose from their seats and walked down the aisle.

I remember hesitating, thinking I was already saved. And then I decided, no, I'm not.

How could God excuse my preoccupation with sexual urges – for I knew by then that's what they were – the church taught me I must think chastely as well as act chastely. Yet sometimes even as I read my Bible, I still gave in to what felt to me like an urgent life force, not a sin. I questioned whether I would be such a "good girl" with men if it weren't for fear of the unknown, the church and my mother. When my sister's friend became pregnant out of wedlock, my mother told my sister not to associate with Marie anymore. She blamed Marie for her 'sin' and not the young man who'd gotten her in trouble. That seemed unjust to me. Still, I longed to be in right relationship with God; I vowed to try harder.

Joining the others, I knelt before the altar, feeling blessed and at peace. The evangelists invited us into an adjoining room to pray together, and talk about what had just happened. And then, to my dismay, they asked us to go immediately to the nearest pay phone and call our parents, wives, husbands, friends, with the good news of our salvation. My elevated mood evaporated. I imagined waking my mother up at ten o'clock to tell her I'd been saved. My mother who had so much religion growing up that she hadn't gone to church for a quarter century.

On Good Friday, David and I meet and walk to a park on Mount Washington that overlooks the city. It feels so good to just sit there and breathe, relaxing in soft southern breezes and the renewed warmth of the sun. After a while, our talk grows deeper as we explore what we see as true in the universe. David raises his head and looks off toward the horizon. "One thing I know for sure," he says fervently, "I truly believe that everything is an idea in the mind of God."

There it is again. The wide gulf between what he has arrived at through years of questioning and study, and my limited world hearing nothing but Bible-based teaching. I realize that he's way beyond the questioning stage and knows what he believes. Since I've never been exposed to the philosophical thought that has so clearly engaged his mind, it's hard for me to understand it even if I want to. My parents encourage us to go to church, but we never discuss religion at home. I certainly don't hear any fresh thinking in my staid Methodist church.

It's never occurred to me to look elsewhere for spiritual answers. What he says frightens me because I don't know what to make of it. It seems like he's reducing everything -- including people -- to a non-material state.

The questions have gotten loose again and I agonize inwardly. Though I grow more and more upset, he doesn't realize anything is wrong. I murmur that I'm a bit tired and want to go home, because I'm in over my head. I have no idea how to talk about this. We walk with our arms about each other, but I feel farther apart from him than ever.

Inside me, the brightness of the day has clouded over. The emotional storm in my soul makes me realize how much I have grown to love David. Feeling we can't be together hurts terribly.

I spend the next day alone in my room, distracted, feeling that I'm about to turn my back on the one person who has seemed to be my ideal life partner. I sit on my bed reviewing our conversation endlessly, but that only sweeps me into a greater vortex of questioning and confusion. My faith has always helped reassure me in the midst of trouble. Now I weep with frustration and sorrow -- it seems as though I must give up either David or what I've believed to be true all my life. As the hours crawl by I don't eat, I don't see anyone. I don't talk with anyone but God. I am in mourning.

Toward evening of that awful day, my mind clears. I begin to question my questions. David has shared with me what he believes; he doesn't say that I must agree with him. Why do I expect him to agree with me? Perhaps there is much we can learn from one another.

I see that the most important way we are alike is in seeking out the essence of the other and caring deeply about that. Slowly I understand that this audacious adventure of staying together will mean recognizing and respecting all the differences, whether they have to do with our world views or our personal imperfections. It means mutual recognition that there is more than one way to believe, and to behave; and more than one path to becoming educated.

Recalling the kindness and thoughtfulness he has always shown, the sense of heaviness lifts from my heart. David is the kind of man I'd always hoped to marry. And he accepts and embraces all that is me: my imperfect body, my uninformed view of life, and my still-searching spirit.

I go to bed that night tired but finally content. I've found the one I love. I'm going to keep him. Two weeks later, when David asks me to marry him, I say 'yes.'

Later that spring, our conversations turn to how wonderful it would be to travel to Paris in August, at the beginning of our life together. But since we earn so little, it seems just wishful thinking. Now that we're engaged, the two of us begin to make tentative plans for the future – including perhaps getting better jobs in New York.

Then we hear that the "Y" will subsidize much of the cost of the Paris trip, if each of us can come up with $200 – a lot of money at that time – plus whatever spending money we want to have. Not only that, we're told there will be one-day layovers in New York, going and coming, time that would allow for job interviews. Once we perceive the dream actually may be possible, we save what we can, borrow from our parents, study a paperback *French Through Pictures*, and start to get really excited.

I sit propped up on my bed at night and tell myself over and over that I am going to Paris. No one in our family has ever done anything like this. It will be me boarding that airplane. I will actually walk the streets of France. For sixteen days, home will be far away. It will give me a chance to interact with people from countries I have only read about; to learn and grow in an entirely different way. I pick up my new black journal with 1955 in golden numerals on the cover and write on the flyleaf:

Thank you, Lord for so many, many things...

For a lifted spirit, and newfound wings---

And the chance to fly!

Fifty-two years later, I sit with that journal beside me. Its spine is broken and tape holds it together, but I'm glad that amazing year is recorded there.

Then something happens we hadn't planned for. I've been working at Pittsburgh Mercantile for about three years. It's been the perfect primer in every facet of ad work. I've been promoted to Fashion Copywriter, laying out my own pages and writing narration for fashion shows. Much as I love the work, by the spring of 1955, I've begun to feel seriously underpaid. I apply for an open copywriting job at Kaufman's, enclosing sample copy that reflects the "Kaufman style" I've studied since I was thirteen. Months go by; I assume the job has been filled. Then, about a week before David and I are due to fly to Paris, I get a call from Kaufman's ad department, telling me I have the job. Stunned, it takes me a few seconds to answer. "Thank you," I say, "I'm happy to hear that! I've wanted to work in Kaufman advertising for years."

I'm told to report on Monday. It'd been nearly five months since I sent in my material. I'd stopped expecting to hear from Kaufman's. So I tell my prospective employer that I've planned a trip to Paris and won't be back until August 25th. Is it possible that I could start after that? A small silence. I know what the answer is going to be.

I try to come up with a way to do both these things I want to do. Then, I break free of disappointment, of indecision. I feel exhilaration instead: Kaufman's chose me out of all its applicants. I have the job if I want it. I'm deciding not to take it.

"I'm sorry," I say. "But I really don't want to change my plans. This trip means a lot to me. Thank you for offering me the job." That exhilaration lasts for days. I've achieved the dream of being considered good enough to write for Kaufmann's. I can do the same for another large company.

The evening before we begin our journey, David and I walk back to my house after receiving communion. In the darkness, I turn my ankle on the steps, but hardly notice it; after the first twinge it stops hurting. I am so happy that nothing bothers me. Not only are we off to Paris the next morning, but we both have job interviews set up – an ad job at Montgomery Ward for me and a research position for David – during the stopover in New York. That night I fall instantly into a deep, contented sleep.

At four in the morning, I'm jolted awake by throbbing pain in my ankle. When I sit up and try to put weight on that foot, I can only sink back on the bed with a groan. Now my sister is stirring. She knows that I need to get on a bus to the airport by mid-morning. Digging in a dresser drawer, she pulls out an elastic bandage she learned how to use in the practical nursing class. Very gently, yet firmly, she wraps my ankle and foot, and helps me get down the stairs. There, despite my protests, she walks me around the kitchen table several times. I remember thinking: I am going to go to Paris, I am. But how?

My sister's quick actions help tremendously; the bandage's support makes the pain bearable. I take some aspirin after breakfast, and dress carefully in my new charcoal cotton suit and white tailored blouse. Pulling stockings up over the bandage is tricky, but in 1955 one doesn't go out without stockings unless to a picnic.

I've called David, and when he and his father come to pick me up, Mr. Will scoops me up in his arms, carries me down several steps and helps me get into the car. In minutes we are headed for the Greyhound bus station downtown.

The TWA flight from New York to Paris lasts seventeen hours. We're traveling in a propeller-driven plane, not a jet. As the slow flight wears on, we nap fitfully. My ankle hurts a bit and I swallow more aspirin. Some of the time, though my eyes are closed, I find myself pondering change and possibility. A year ago, I couldn't have imagined making this trip abroad. I had no idea how to make connections in New York and interview there for a job. Leaving Pittsburgh seemed very remote. Now I feel suspended in midair in more ways than one -- floating between Part One and Part Two of my life. I open my eyes and gaze out the window from my middle seat. We are flying above the clouds at 17,000 feet. Though I've never been on a plane before, the cloud carpet looks familiar; it reminds me of

Mount Washington and my fogged-in childhood. I wonder what awaits me on the other side of the world.

At Orly Airport, our Pittsburgh group leader calls out names, shepherding us onto a bus that will take us to our lodgings. I am to stay at a private girls' school on the Boulevard San Michel. David and several other men from our group are billeted a few blocks away at the Lycee St. Louis, once used as a military barracks.

My Swedish room-mate is unpacking when I arrive; grinning, she comes over and clasps my hands. For the first time in my life, I discover that my English is useless. But it doesn't matter. Laughing, we mouth our names, pick up objects, point and gesture, warming to each other right away. Over the next sixteen days, as we sleep and undress a few feet away from each other, I learn that friendship isn't based on language.

Each morning, David and I meet for croissants and jus de pamplemouse (grapefruit juice) at a little cafe nearby. Then we join a conference work group, talking through interpreters with some of the young men and women who have come here from more than ninety countries. There is searching discussion about what's going on in the world just now: War, conscription, the hydrogen bomb, what real security might look like. Some say they have spoken with twenty-year-olds who are so frightened that they fall into apathy, lacking all sense of purpose. Group leaders emphasize that we need to witness to our

Christian faith by reaching out to lonely, confused young people no matter where we live. There is enthusiastic sharing of programs that are working; new ideas worth pondering and acting upon. I listen carefully, and wonder what I could possibly do when I return, to build on what I'm learning. My small church doesn't have any "outreach programs" and I doubt if there's room in its budget to start one, anyway, to implement their ideas.

As David and I walk the city, we turn a corner and stop before a weathered memorial plaque commemorating those who died fighting the Germans during the liberation in 1944. Though normalcy has returned to Paris, there are reminders everywhere that World War II is a raw and recent memory for its people. We Americans have simply had to get used to food shortages and hang dark window shades. But close to a decade and a half ago, on June 14, 1940, Hitler's army marched down these avenues and completely invaded these people's lives. The Nazi occupation lasted four numbing years, making Parisians prisoners in their own city. In the Palais des Sports, the huge arena where our larger meetings are held, another plaque states that during the occupation, several hundred Jews were held there before being sent off to concentration camps, where many perished. There is something stark and humbling about standing where they stood, unwilling to give up, hoping against hope to somehow survive the consequences of hate.

In the evening, we love to walk beside the Seine, watching the reflected lights of Paris glimmering in the river's swells. As we stroll there one warm Sunday night, I have news to share with David. Grabbing his hand, I try to describe the strange experience I'd had earlier that day:

Since there's still time before we are to meet, I take the elevator to the roof of the girl's school, and stand there, transfixed. How beautiful it is! All around me, stretching in every direction, I see the pastel rooftops of the Left Bank -- dusty pinks, blues, pale lemon yellows. I feel surrounded by a magnificent painting without a frame – and I am part of the painting. It sounds strange, but it is the closest thing to a vision I've ever had.

Later, as we sit, staring at the Seine, I remind David how I've been agonizing because all this education is going to be wasted on me, that I won't be able to do anything with it.

"Maybe I won't be able to use the nuts and bolts," I muse. "But in every session, we hear from folks who're moving from despair to hope. The programs they're describing help people to become something else, something better. They're talking about transformation."

Surrounded by the still darkness, we hear only the warm slap of water a few feet from where we sit. But I'm back there in the sunlight on the roof, not understanding what was happening, but knowing something was. Something important. David puts his arm around me as I struggle to convey my feelings. "When I saw this artist's view of the city, full of order and color, and felt myself a part of it, I understood why there's no frame -- it's a work in progress. And then I thought, maybe I'm here to experience transformation myself."

David squeezes my shoulder and we sit for a few moments, pondering what I've shared, wondering what it means.

"There are all kinds of conversion experiences, Ros. I think that's what you had up there. Trying to discover who God is isn't enough; we have to figure out who we are and where we fit into the universe. That's why books have been so valuable to me."

"For me, being with people I can talk to is even better," I say. "I need to hear their stories, recognize how different their lives may be from mine."

I tell him how tired I am of being boxed in by my parents' prejudices. And that I'm realizing my folks probably grew up with the ideas they had because they never had a chance to really get to know people that were different. Nodding, David agrees, looking thoughtful. "Since we've been here it occurred to me you might want to take a look at some books I have about different religions—we could read them out loud together." We get up and resume walking, loving the quiet and our closeness. I'm so relieved that he understands what I've been telling him. Yesterday, I might have said I wasn't interested in reading those books. Today I am.

On our last day in Paris, we gather once again in the huge Palais des Sports. Everyone is provided with earphones to receive translation of the closing presentations. While we wait for the program to begin, I study the wide variety of faces, of colorings, of dress, and demeanor. How glad I am that we're not all the same; this way the world is so much more interesting. I think of the wounds the city has endured and wonder at the roots of malevolence that created the Nazis, who believed they were a race superior to all others. I remember my father telling us when he was young, he'd been invited to join the Ku Klux Klan; he didn't, he said, even though he was in sympathy with them, because he didn't want to kill anyone.

The celebratory program begins, perhaps with a few too many grand and optimistic words for the pensive mood I'm in. And then, the organist sounds the stirring chords of a familiar hymn, signaling that the conference is drawing to a close. Rising as one, we raise our many-stranded voice, singing in Spanish and English, German and French, accents of the Netherlands and African nations and Asia: "Now thank we all our God, with hands and heart and voices…"

On our return flight to New York, I feel grateful for this time of fellowship with those not willing to be satisfied with the status quo. That's the kind of person I want to be. I feel I've gotten a different education than the one I got in school. All of us have been challenged by the differences in people, and astonished again and again by our sameness. Most of all, I'll cherish the gifts of kindness and curiosity and hope I've been given. Encountering another world, I think, offers wisdom for living in the one I inhabit.

Mid-flight, my thoughts slowly return to the interview I had with Mr. O'Brien when we stopped in New York two weeks ago. He still had other applicants to see, so I will need to check back at Montgomery Ward during the layover. Who knows, I may be leaving my familiar Pittsburgh world behind for good, to live and work in New York. It will seem another sort of 'foreign' country in a way, to someone from a small neighborhood overlooking a bustling city. Even a year ago, I wouldn't have felt able to make that transition. Now, I feel ready.

Mr. O'Brien ushers me into his office, asking me how the Paris trip went. Sitting there, feeling a bit tired from the long plane trip, I wonder if he's going to say the position has been taken. Then he reminds me that I'd made a point of saying I hadn't gone to college, and asks if I feel that will be a drawback in any way.

I look at him, and think, he's on my side.

When I reply that I feel my copywriting experience is what has readied me for this position and I don't think college is necessary for it, his blue eyes twinkle and he laughs. "Good! If you don't think you need it, neither do we." I smile back, and allow myself to breathe in the import of his words. I have the job. Yes! I have the job!

On the bus with David, going back to Pittsburgh, I review the rest of my meeting with Mr. O'Brien. I'll be making $78 for a 35-hour week, nearly twice what I made at my old job. I'll be writing catalog copy, and the buyers will bring the merchandise to our office for us to examine—no chasing after buyers! I sigh, for now just glad to be going home, but thinking, this is going to be a good move.

Every so often during my September train ride to New York, my aura of excitement slips a bit, and worries begin to pop up. I wish David were with me, but he wasn't able to find a job at the same time I did, and won't be joining me for a week or so. If only I weren't such a worrier. Despite my brave face for Mr. O'Brien, and regardless of my achievements so far, the old coil of fear begins to move restlessly in the pit of my stomach. It looks like the gargoyles have boarded with me. I swallow and look around the train car at the carefully closed and guarded faces. How many of them, I wonder, at each new stage of their lives, are afraid of failure? Are they terrified, too, by the thought of reinvention?

At the end of the long, lonesome first week, I'm in the communal bath room of Spellman Hall YWCA. Leaning over, I massage shampoo into my hair, thinking how strange it is to do this at the busy row of sinks where six other women are using blow-driers and rinsing out underwear. Outside in the corridor, someone's phone code is ringing—two long rings and a short. Over all of it pours the sweet-sad melody of "Autumn Leaves" on somebody's portable radio. The music wraps around me as I squeeze water from my hair and grab my towel. I miss David more than ever.

The next morning when I pass the desk downstairs, the clerk tells me I have two phone messages. I'd completely forgotten to listen for my phone code. David is in New York and has been trying to get in touch with me. He'll be here to meet me in a couple of hours. The tightly wound spring within me relaxes. I've been feeling overwhelmed trying to adjust to strange streets and impatient subway doors, curt answers and wrong directions. Now I won't be alone against the newness.

My second week on the job at Montgomery Ward, I'm thrilled that my co-workers invite me to lunch with them. We take the elevator down to a little restaurant on the ground floor of the Varick Street building where we work. We manage to claim the last available window table and they quickly decide on tuna salad sandwiches. Ordering scrambled eggs and tea, I find myself thinking, how come we never ate tuna at home? I don't even know if I like it. My companions wave hello and briefly speak to someone they know at another table. I sit quietly, watching how they behave in their universe. Sue, the tall dark one, wears that little secret smile of the newly engaged (I know it well) and talks excitedly about an ivory satin gown with tiny seed pearls, and her plans for a big fancy wedding in the spring. Nancy is blonde and petite. I've already learned about her passion for performing in small theatre productions. Now she's chattering about her latest gig. I listen, wondering at the vast difference between the lives and expectations of these young women and my friends in Pittsburgh. As the conversation turns to plays on Broadway, Nancy asks me if I've seen Ibsen's "A Doll's House."

I stare at her, fork in midair, realizing that I don't have a clue what she's talking about. David and I see a movie once a week and, on our budget, that's about it. But it isn't just that the price of a Broadway ticket is out of our league; we haven't grown up with the idea that play-going is something one routinely does. I've never heard of Ibsen or his plays, and haven't become socially aware enough yet to hide my ignorance. I may not need more education to do my job, but my social and cultural knowledge is going to need some work. During the next few months, as we get to know each other better, I let them see that the culture of New York City is very different from the small-town one I've known; that it's going to take a long while for me to acclimate myself. We gradually relax and talk about things each of us can relate to.

The office everyday becomes routine. I get better at counting type characters of different fonts and sizes so that my copy will fit the catalog layout; discover where and how far ahead of pub date to get merchandise information. I learn to like my immediate boss, who drinks too much coffee and works too much overtime; but have trouble warming up to her boss, who is harsh and unpredictable. I love getting a decent salary, employee discount, and health coverage, but see right away that here I won't be able to write imaginative, Kaufman-style copy. This job is not about creativity. The most important thing to Montgomery Ward is whether the copy I compose has the required product information and settles nicely into a space two and a half inches wide and one inch deep.

The days grow shorter, leaden clouds gather and the sun is a pale wash of yellow on cold, gray streets. It's hard being unattached souls with no permanent home in a fast-paced city like New York. It doesn't occur to us to simply live together; for us, living together means being married. How wonderful it will be, we think, to have a small apartment, where the two of us can sit in our sock-feet and read the paper together; knowing that when we look up, we'll see each other just a few feet away. Now David has a full time job so we talk about setting a wedding date. We'll be married in Pittsburgh at my Methodist Church on New Year's Eve in the morning.

Making plans long-distance is tougher than we thought. We want a simple church wedding with a reception for close friends and relatives at my family's home afterwards. But there are so many questions: Will we ask the choir to sing? Shall we employ the imperious regular organist or the substitute one whom I have grown to like? With only a week to spend in Pittsburgh, will we have enough time to get our blood tests there—three days before the wedding—as required by law?

On the Saturday morning after Thanksgiving, I get down to Klein's at 14th Street and Fifth Avenue right after they open. I don't have enough money for a real wedding dress, but figure they might just have something appropriate, maybe even among the mark-downs. Walking slowly among racks crammed with dresses I could never wear, I search for something street-length but very, very special. All of a sudden, I see a silky, cream-colored dress with delicate gold-brushed flowers -- unbelievably my size. The cut is elegantly simple: V-neck, narrow waist, full skirt. Holding my breath, I turn over the tag, and gasp—it had been $40, but now is half-price. That means I can afford a small ivory hat to go with it.

Meanwhile, my mother writes to let me know that our rather sudden decision to marry has put a crimp in their budget. Less than three months away from home, I've forgotten so much I should have remembered. I know she never goes anywhere where she needs a 'dress-up' dress, so now she must buy one. I know my blue-collar father doesn't own a suit or dress shoes (they have to special-order the size 15 that he needs), so that is another unexpected outlay. I feel guilty that our tiny, informal church wedding, purposely kept as no-frills as possible, has still caused them financial distress. Should we have gone to a Justice of the Peace, alone in New York City? We both want our families to be part of this important day.

I think now that there may have been more causing my mother's upset than concern over money. Unspoken, but hidden there under the little pile of complaints in her letter, I sensed her usual worry over any kind of social event in which she would have to assume a more visible role. I realize too, looking back, that she may have been concerned about my physical health, taking on marriage and perhaps, too soon, a family. She was actually right to worry, as having children at a rapid pace was to affect my well-being considerably—something no doctor warned me about until I was about to have my fourth child, thirteen years later.

It is cold and snowing lightly on the Saturday morning of our wedding, December 31, 1955. David's father drives me the few blocks to Mt. Washington Methodist Church. I'm wearing my warm red everyday Chesterfield coat over the ivory dress from Klein's sale rack. Black plastic rain boots keep my shoes dry. Slowly, I walk up the steps and into the church where I've been a member since I was eleven years old. I know every nook and cranny of it, from the kindergarten room to the bell tower. How odd it seems now to be back here in this place that's been like a second home, knowing I may never step inside again.

As the old organ heralds the beginning of our wedding ceremony, I wonder what is going through my parents' minds, especially my father's, as he stands quietly waiting to walk me down the aisle. I'm the younger daughter of his second family, the one who learned the names of wrenches and pliers when I was five so I could hand him tools when he was down under the chassis of his Model A Ford. I'm the daughter he taught at seven how to knead the soft, pink clay-like wallpaper cleaner, and to work it in a circular fashion to clean the floral patterned wallpaper from the baseboard up to my shoulders, while he worked from there to the ceiling. In the thirties, I would sit and listen with him to the Friday night radio boxing matches between Joe Louis and Max Schmeling, and to the Saturday afternoon country music programs that my mother hated. When did I start pulling away? How was it that he became a stranger—working nights, sleeping days—and coming home drunk on paydays? The week before I left in September, I had put down my fork one night at the dinner table, not stopping the bile I felt rising from my gut to my tongue, furiously letting him know how much pain his drinking had inflicted on us all, and that I couldn't wait to get away from it. As the organ nears the cue for us to walk forward, I don't remember feeling much relief after that outburst. The look of stunned realization that crossed his face made me wish I hadn't spoken. Standing stiffly now in his new blue suit, waiting to cradle my arm as we take our last walk together, he must be painfully aware of me now as the daughter for whom despair of his ever changing suddenly became too heavy a burden to bear.

And my mother is sitting with my sister in a pew up front, perhaps feeling uncomfortable in her floral rayon dress that's too dark to be becoming, but probably what she could afford. Is she picturing the kids coming too fast and too close? Is she thinking that I'll end up trapped in the same kind of forced domesticity as hers? Or worse, is she worried that I'll have difficult pregnancies because of the scoliosis? She may even share my secret concern about getting along with a college-educated husband. I wish there had been time for us to have a long, quiet talk; time for her to tell me how she's feeling about all of this. Is she happy for me? Or does she think I'm making a mistake? Our family's habit of not expressing what we feel is still operating, even on my wedding day.

As the organ music builds, every worrisome thought drops away. My father and I walk toward the altar, where David waits to make me his wife. The cross high above the chancel glows, as I remember it glowing every Sunday since I was a child. I pray I'll be able to meet whatever comes in this new life.

Later on, at the reception, I notice that my mother is very withdrawn. Hovering wraithlike near the festive table, her face is pale and tired. I hope she isn't getting sick, and think briefly of asking her if she wants to go up and lie down. But I know she will say her place is there on my wedding day. In the midst of my happiness, I decide there's no way I can fix everything; she's never been comfortable hosting occasions like this, and will probably be fine when it's over. Over the tiny man and woman on top of the wedding cake my new husband and I smile at each other—and embrace the sweetness of our wedding day.

We didn't plan on having a honeymoon. We can't afford it and don't really need it. Anyway, we sort of had a honeymoon in Paris— before we got married. In a day or two, we return to New York. I go back to work at Ward's, but David has been laid off by the retail store where he was working--How could he even think of asking for vacation time at Christmas? – so he begins looking for another job.

Slowly, we settle into our furnished, fifth-floor walkup on West 89th Street, not concerned at first about the sagging bed and closet-sized kitchen. I love the bohemian look of the place: a spacious living room with a huge front window, two sofas, a gently-faded carpet, a small table and a chair or two. We are together, in our first home.

During our engagement, right up until our wedding night, we've never had intercourse. But we have explored each other's bodies. Clothing acted as both aphrodisiac and safety valve. It did not deter us from caressing hollows and pleasuring swells; we tasted, inhaled, memorized. Now we don't have to tell ourselves to stop. It's finally okay to follow this pleasure to its conclusion. Lying with him at night, I'm warmed by the knowledge that he loves my whole being, imperfections and all. We arouse each other with loving caresses, but have trouble actually having sex; the consummation of marriage is difficult if the partners know little about the intricacies of the subject. I'm about five foot seven to his six foot two and though we fit together beautifully in loving embrace, it takes us a while to get much farther than that. I imagine our experience might have been like that of many just-married people at that time; all of our young lives, there was no dependable birth control. We'd been frightened into being chaste, and didn't know how to undo those years of prohibition.

Somewhere in the autumn of 1956, I come home from work and see my sister's stationery through the metal grill of the mailbox. My mother has been having tests; I wonder if there's any news. Dropping my bag, I tear the envelope open before even putting my key into the inside door. The first line punches me hard in the stomach:

"Dear Ros, Mother has leukemia. She's in the hospital."

I struggle through the heavy door, and up four flights to my apartment, hanging onto the banister hard because I can't see where I'm going. Inside, it takes a few minutes to refocus my blurred eyes on the rest of the short note. The doctors don't know much more yet. My sister is alone and not sure what to expect. She's scared and wants me to come home. I sit on the bed with the letter in my hand as the long day slowly becomes yesterday. How strange it is that we think our mothers will always be there, a living, breathing connection to the nothingness from which we came. I am both pained and numb, lost in some odd place I've never been before. I don't pick up the half-read novel, or feel a need for food. As the night gathers about me, its usual friendly embrace has changed to a vast emptiness. There are so many questions and only blanks where the answers should be. My mother is going to die. How soon? How can I go to work tomorrow when my mother might be dying? Will I lose my job if I take some days off? Should I care about that now?

Cold moonlight pales the sheets next to me, the space where David usually would be. He's already in Pittsburgh to take a test for his master's degree at Pitt. I haven't been able to call him because we still can't afford a phone. Finally, after only an hour or two of fitful sleep, I dig in pockets to gather some change and head out to find a pay phone. When I finally walk shakily into the office, Sue sees right away something is up. "My mother's really sick. I hope they'll let me go home." I barely get out the words before I start crying again and she wraps me in her arms. "Of course you can go home. Let's go see Bessie."

By mid-afternoon I am on a Greyhound bus, dry-eyed, not knowing what awaits in Pittsburgh. As the hours announce themselves by where the hazy sun sits in the sky, I drift from looking out the window to the deep sleep of exhaustion; then wake again to the dread memory of where I am going and why. I reflect that my mother was rarely ever sick as I was growing up; maybe her strong constitution will stand up to this onslaught. Then I wonder how long it will be before she doesn't feel like herself anymore, and I hope they will have something to give her if it hurts. Late that night, I stumble into the house that no longer seems mine, and fall into a restless sleep.

When David and I go to visit my mother in South Side Hospital, she's sitting up in bed and looks cheered to see me. I can tell by her manner that she doesn't feel terribly sick yet, but she has to be worried by the diagnosis. She doesn't speak of it though, talks instead about getting back to normalcy.

"I'll be going home soon, and they say I can keep on doing little things around the house like sewing or hand washing. Your sister's going to get some time off to help me more."

There is such an unreal quality to the hour I spend with her. Even though she's five feet eight, she looks small and thin lying here in this big white bed. How not herself she seems. My mother was always doing. Always planning a little ahead. She'd be mixing up biscuits, or filling the house with the smell of her thick potato soup with onions. Some years my father would go out into the country and bring home bushels of elderberries and baskets of corn for her to put up jam and piccalilli. Every October, like clockwork, she and my Aunt Nell would pile all the old china, gravy boats, and baking pans on the gray formica kitchen table, with the extra leaf put in to hold it all. Then they'd clean out the built-in china closet with soap and water top to bottom, and put all the sparkling clean things we kids helped wash back in – we loved this ritual because we knew it was part of getting ready for holiday pie-making and turkey roasting.

An aide comes in to take my mother's blood pressure and my mind snaps back to the too-bright room, the gleaming metal bars on the bed. I stifle the flood of memories. It's almost October. My mother won't be doing those things ever again.

"I'm so glad you're going to be able to go home in a few days, Mother. You'll have your cat and all your familiar things around you, rather than being here with people coming in and out and noise in the hall all night." She says that doesn't bother her because they give her a sleeping pill, but I know better. What she really wants is to walk back into her own house and sit in her rocker with a good book.

After we visit a little longer, she admits that she tires more easily these days and needs to take short naps. As we get ready to leave, I realize that through the whole time we've been there, she hasn't complained once. My mother isn't about to change now; she's always been a proud, stoic, practical woman. Still, I see in her eyes that she hates the rude intrusion of leukemia into her life, a struggle she can hope to outlast but never control. Going down in the elevator, I wonder if I will ever see her again.

At Christmastime, I sit with David beneath the vast cathedral arches of Riverside Church, lost in the magnificent chords of the great organ. I ponder what it must have been like to be Mary, long ago, informed by an angel that she would give birth to a holy being. I hope that soon I will be able to have my own baby. It will be a holy event for me, as well.

A few weeks later, I discover that I am pregnant.

I feel the familiar combination of emotions when big new things happen: happiness, excitement, and more than a little apprehension. One doctor had told me a few years before that scoliosis conditions may interfere with carrying a baby to term. Now, I go to see an elderly Italian doctor who checks me head to toe, declares me basically healthy, and gives me injections "to build up my womb." After measuring the width of my hips, "No, no," he says, "you should have no problem at all." He doesn't notice, and I haven't realized, that my tailbone is skewed inward. Was this the product of the boy pulling the chair out from under me when I was twelve? Or is this part of the scoliosis? Whatever the cause, it will create a problem.

Morning sickness settles over me each day, sometimes so bad that I can't stand the smell of an apple sitting on my desk. As the six month mark approaches, I decide Ward's is going to have to do without me.

My doctor has said he'll be using ether, applied off and on at first to ease the pain and then steadily so I'll be out during the actual birth. He has warned me not to eat just before coming to the hospital, because the combination of food and ether could make me nauseous. What I haven't foreseen is that I will be in mild labor all through the night and part of the morning -- fourteen hours -- before the pains start coming close enough to go to the hospital. I am tired and weak from not eating, so during the first hour after I arrive there, my pains increase but my pushing accomplishes nothing. The doctor finally examines me manually, and realizes the tailbone is interfering with progress. I'm put to sleep while he delivers my firstborn with the aid of forceps.

"Mrs. Will, wake up. You have a little girl." The nurse's loud voice pokes through the fog of my anesthesia. I struggle to answer but my tongue feels thick and out of order. "Is she alright?" "Fine and healthy, Mrs. Will!" "Thank God," I manage, and fall gratefully back into the mist.

Lindsay is an easy baby, but I am not an easy mother. My place in my parents' home had been the second child, the baby sister. They took care of me. I've never taken care of anybody. What do I know about parenting? I lay my little one on her back because I'm afraid she will smother on her stomach. Then I worry that she will choke on a burp, so I turn her on her side, propped with a pillow. We don't have a diaper service at first and I soak the dirty ones in the bath tub. I consult my Dr. Spock book on baby care so much that the paperback starts to fall apart before Lindsay reaches six months. We buy another one.

The phone rings late one evening, when Lindsay is less than a month old. There's a strange quaver in my mother's voice. I hold my breath, thinking she's going to say the leukemia is worse. But she tells me instead that my father has been in an auto accident. His car hit the soft shoulder of a country road, and rolled down an embankment. His chest is crushed. A question dies unspoken as she goes on.

"Rosalyn, your father is dead." A moment passes before I can speak. My throat grows tight with regret as I realize how much I want to talk with him again. I tell my mother I will try to come for the funeral but am not sure how we're going to manage that. We have so little money for anything extra. The baby is so small. Somehow, we decide we will both go home for my father's funeral, and take Lindsay with us.

My sister has helped make arrangements for the funeral and the reception afterward, but my mother seems pretty frail. Since she's been sick, she has decided to have her hair cut short and permanent-waved so that it's easier to care for. She no longer looks like my mother. We go through the surreal process of talking to folks who come to see my father laid out at the funeral home. Most of the visitors are people from the Methodist church who don't know my father or my mother, but come to comfort my sister and me. They have trouble knowing what to say. So do we.

Willing myself to stand by the open casket for a few moments, I try to say goodbye to my father. Although the hard memories are still with me, I tell him I forgive him, and pray that he can forgive me for yelling at him. Because there's nothing more to say, I relieve my sister, who has been standing by the entrance to the viewing room.

Soon I greet a young man who looks familiar to me, but I can't come up with a name. He looks beyond me to the casket, agony in his eyes. "I'm Richard Baker. That man there is my father." A friend of Richard's just happened to see the notice in a local paper, and he had driven for hours in his truck to get there from Kentucky. I'll learn later that my family hadn't called him because they couldn't find his phone number. My half-brother and I, my father's son and daughter who barely know each other, stand there looking at this man who died too soon, and back at one another, wordlessly mourning all that might have been.

Four months later, in January, 1958, I travel alone back to Pittsburgh. My mother is gone. I have no name for the bottomless emptiness I feel. Pictures of my grandparents never had meaning for me because they died before I could know them. Now, on the edge of learning to understand my father and mother better, they too are gone. I seem to be walking in a strange land where I don't know the language, and I'm lost.

As I go through the draining vigil once more with my sister, I feel keenly the severing of a connection I had always thought would be there. Who will help me now with questions about my children, about…life? In the car after the funeral, I sit weary and dry-eyed as we drive home to my in-laws' house. David's mother puts her arm around me and says, "I'm just realizing that in the last couple of years, Rosalyn, you've become a bride, a mother, and an orphan." As the truth of her words sinks in, I am oddly grateful. Somehow, I've turned a corner in the bleak, unfamiliar landscape and find myself back home. Surrounded again by love, I let myself grieve.

Over the next few years, my body surprises me. It turns out to be incredibly fertile, responsive, and strong. After Lindsay, I have two more children before my twenty-eighth birthday and another one eight years later. When my first is born, I have no idea that I am embarking on more than two decades of intense mothering. Before that time is up, I will wake up in the night -- like a newborn -- longing for nurture.

Mind

In the middle of making dinner, I see my husband sitting on the sofa, leafing through a New School catalog. Just looking at the bright Spring '72 cover depresses me. It represents the freedom to stretch one's mind, a freedom that hasn't been a significant part of my life for a very long time.

A few months before, Lindsay was writing a high school biology paper on how the embryo recreates evolution in the womb. Right now she's got little pieces of paper scattered all over her bedroom floor for her upcoming report explaining how the Electoral College works. Julie fills notebooks with poetry and has just put together an aluminum dustpan in her junior high metal shop. Eric, in 6th grade, is bringing home achievement awards for his drawing and poster contest entries. Three-year-old Scott learned how to count and built his vocabulary from watching Sesame Street. And David has moved steadily up at the National Board of the YWCA, from statistical clerk to research analyst, and continues taking college courses on the side.

And what have I been learning? Patience. For years now, I've worked at learning patience. Isn't that what mothers do? My brain cells are congealing oatmeal on the side of an unstirred pot. Something has to change. I'm itching to fly.

That night, I stand at our second floor kitchen window, leaning out into the dark with my elbows resting on the sill. The yellow brightness of the kitchen and my day's work are behind me. I'm surprised to find the night crying softly, just as I am. What is that line from Thoreau? "The mass of men lead lives of quiet desperation." Women, too, I think, women, too. Breathing in the chill dampness, I am strangely comforted. The night understands, without my saying a word. I sigh and turn back to the kitchen to put the dishes away.

For fifteen years, I've pushed aside nearly every activity except being a wife and mother. I heat bottles of formula in the dim early morning kitchen; run to the store in the rain for medicine; listen to grumbles about who did what to whom first; bandage skinned knees and sooth wounded feelings; sympathize with husbandly complaints about the job and the constant lack of money. I cook and clean when I feel inept at one and hate the other. I guess I'm like my mother, in some ways, who determined to do the best she could in whatever situation she found herself. I learned as a child that she sat up nights holding me in her arms near steaming pots of water to ease the whooping cough I'd had when I was two. She tried hard to feed us well on a small budget, paid attention to our growing–up troubles, even showed up on rare occasions at school on our behalf, which I know was difficult for her. Like her I, too, rebel against the idea that motherhood and keeping house are the ultimate aspirations for women, sufficient to keep us mentally and spiritually nourished all our lives. I remember coming home from high school many days to see her lying in the dark living room, nursing a migraine. She'd wanted so much that never happened.

So what am I to do with this tempest brewing inside me? Wasn't I thrilled that this gentle, funny guy wanted to marry me? Wasn't I relieved and happy when I learned that my scoliosis wouldn't keep me from having children? Yes, and yes. Then what is my problem? Why am I crying because the night outside my window seems to represent freedom, and I have to turn away? The answer feathers along the far edges of my mind like the words of a long forgotten song; I tease it slowly to clarity. It isn't that I don't want to be a wife and mother; I just crave something else besides -- I long to be Rosalyn again.

Where am I?
That part of me that is truly myself?
Not that which grows impatient with a seven-year-old's questions,
Nor that, weary with being tested by teenage independence,
But the me that was there, before all that—
Before the stained shirts and broken book bags and noisy TV.
I was an artist.
I wrote poetry and music.
I was a person who listened to the pain of others
And sometimes could help.
I had friends.

I was a friend.

Now I flounder in chores and busyness,

The years of nurturing stretch behind and before:

My friends are other mothers, trying to remember who they are.

Am I to disappear altogether?

Or will these pieces of me return

At some later time—

Shadowy and hesitant—

Like an embryo, ready to grow from nothing

To something.

Someone.

Me.

The next day when I tell David how I'm feeling, he asks if I'd like to take a class instead of him – we can't manage for both of us to go. It's time, I think. This is something I need to do. While David helps the kids with their homework, I look through the catalog, imagining how it might be to take this course or that one. But I know what I hunger for.

The poetry course will begin in early April. For weeks, I am excited and afraid and happy; I am a crocus sticking its head up, hoping it won't snow again. David has volunteered to shepherd the kids for eight Saturday mornings. That is a gift in itself.

This is going to be some experiment. It will demand creativity of someone who hasn't shown much of it lately. Off and on in the sixties, I wrote some anti-war poetry. Some of these David or I set to music. One day I sent off a song called "It's Not Too Late" to Pete Seeger, the passionate anti-war folk singer our family had long listened to and loved. He wrote back that he'd sent it on to a publication called *Broadside*. David surprised me with a copy when I was in the hospital after giving birth to Scott. There was our song on page two:

One day soon, the sons of men shall reach the moon—

Do we suppose that love is found upon a star?

Here below, a man hates men he does not know---

Does he imagine things will change up there so far?

We dare to fly into uncharted skies

But will not listen to a brother's cries.

Worlds apart, we try to change all but the heart

And if debate should fail, our guns are near at hand.

It's not too late, the moon and stars have got to wait---

The space between us is what we must understand.

Later on, I updated those words to take into account the moon landing, but what was happening in the world in the late sixties was truly scary. The leaders I loved and trusted were getting shot, one after the other: President John Kennedy, his brother, Robert Kennedy, the Reverend Martin Luther King, Jr., Medgar Evers. The country I believed in was fighting a war in Vietnam that many Americans thought was wrong. Because part of our taxes went to support the war effort, we considered expatriating and David went up to Canada twice hoping to find work, but nothing was available. Now it's 1972 and that war is still going on. Sometimes I wonder if it'll still be roaring along when my older son reaches draft age. In a month, he'll turn 11. He was three when it started.

There have been some balmy days in among the cold ones lately – the incredibly earnest kind of days that make me feel restless and moody. Suddenly, the air is soft and the yellow-green haze on trees sprouts into tender leaves overnight.

But what am I going to wear to this poetry class? Since I haven't worked for three years, I wear flannel shirts and threadbare sweaters around the house. Luckily, I have a couple of loose-fitting, well-cut sweaters to wear to church. But now it's getting warmer.

The next afternoon I pull out of the closet the few decent things I haven't worn since last spring. My rose wool suit would be perfect —but when I try it on I'm shocked to see that the boxy jacket with its beautiful suede ties now fits too tightly over the worsening curve of my spine. The polka-dotted blue dress looks springy, but I can't even button it because my back takes up more space than it used to. I'd loved both these outfits and thought I would wear them for years. Holding them up as if deciding to buy them all over again, I think how fortunate I've been to find affordable clothes that made me feel happy and confident despite my scoliosis. What am I going to do now? How on earth am I going to find clothes to fit me? As I put the suit and dress back on their hangers, knowing I won't be wearing them anymore, a huge sob rips through my body. I bend over with the ache of it, hugging them close to me. My days of pretending I can look normal are over. For school, I end up wearing a sweater and pants.

But I see I've got a much bigger problem than what to wear to poetry class.

The closer the date of the first class comes, the more worried I get. I've been in the house so much, that it's come to be my safe haven. It's time for me to inch out of the familiar wrappings of the housewife chrysalis I've gotten used to hiding in. How am I going to manage in a roomful of college-educated people? What if I have to stand up and read my poetry in front of the class? Sometimes I'm even afraid I'll take the wrong train, or not be able to find the classroom. But this is something I want to do. I have to do it. Attending the class will make me write poetry, maybe some of it better than any I've ever written. Being able to create something means so much to me right now. That moment when the "quiet desperation" line came into my head was one among many just like it, but I hadn't put words to the feeling before. The fact that those words seem to fit my situation so perfectly is frightening.

My first class day, I arrive early, and gaze around with delight at the ivory walled room blessed with windows; the corner one is already cracked to give us fresh air. April sunshine pools softly on the row of seats nearby. A poster portrait of Walt Whitman hovers like a benevolent angel just above where I sit near the opposite wall. Other writers: Shakespeare, Coleridge, Thoreau, Dickinson—a preponderance of men—haunt the room. An interesting mix of people slowly enters: young and older, more women than men; some looking confident, others, clearly nervous. I am no longer apprehensive, but anxious to begin.

Pearl London walks into the room wearing a gentle smile, as though she knows that we will discover something wonderful together in the next few weeks. For a few minutes, she sits quietly at the desk, drawing us into her world, as we begin to position her in ours. She is middle-aged, her curling dark hair lightly touched with grey. Her navy suit is simple, well-cut. We are all immediately engaged by her eyes as she stands and declares, "Poetry is a way of seeing." Inviting us to entertain possibility, she distributes envelopes in which are paper cutouts of a hand, and asks us to ponder these for a moment. During the next fifteen minutes we are to come up with some sort of imagery that shapes itself around the hand.

How precious are these moments of potential: the playing with an idea, the allowance of time for such a frivolous and delightful purpose, the importance placed on what each of us produces because it is uniquely our own. As I bend over my work, all the blood in my body seems rushing to my head to jump-start my brain. Yet it doesn't take me long to begin; the words seem already there, waiting for this moment.

Though I feel a familiar migraine developing, I struggle to stay focused as a few courageous students volunteer to read their work. I marvel at the amazing range of perceptions generated by that one simple shape: We have demonstrated a dozen very individual "ways of seeing." After class, I speak to one of the poets, an older man whose poem has moved me tremendously. Stepping outside, we are buffeted by a freshened wind, and duck into a diner for a hot drink. He is a shy man, yet seems to sense that speaking of his pain will help to ease it. He tells me of being beaten by his parents as a child, how he would run to an abandoned house in the neighborhood, sob out his grief and slowly recover himself. The house always welcomed him in its quiet embrace. It became his mother and father.

He has freed himself, I thought. I wonder if I can do the same.

That evening, I start putting down on the page my own frustration, anger, feelings of nothingness; the neglected pieces of my psyche that I often haven't realized were aching for attention. I begin the long journey of writing my fragmented self back together again.

Later that year, I start working part-time at Gimbels East. During the rest of the seventies, I sign up for courses that have to do with changing my life: a New York University class in Public Relations, a Career Internships course at Womanschool. I discover there are other women weary of being at home; some have married right out of college and never entered the workplace. Now they're unsure what, if anything, they have to offer in the work world. I'm grateful now for my early work experience. Hungrily, I draw sustenance from each course, gaining confidence, sharpening what I already know how to do.

These changes in my life mirror shifts in our family life. We see a counselor to help sort out teenage -- and midlife -- transitions. The older kids don't say much about my going to classes; mostly their thoughts and troubles are connected with school. In our cramped four-and-a-half room apartment, there have begun to be boundary problems. David and I need time to be alone, without the children. As we all begin to understand each other better, the kids realize I could use their help with dishes and room straightening. We buy a small TV they can watch in their bedroom in the evenings. Lindsay decides to deliver newspapers to pay for her guitar lessons. Eventually, all will seek paper routes to earn pocket money. David does heavier chores like the laundry now, and bigger shopping trips in between my little ones.

And then David's mother offers again to help us with the down payment on a house. I've dragged my feet on this, afraid of not being able to take proper care of a house. Now we decide to make the move. Instead of experiencing a greater burden, I feel freer than I've felt in years. There's a little yard where I can garden. The kids are still near their friends. David and I have a bedroom again – with a door. Slowly, the tangled filaments of constant homemaking begin to loosen; I slip out of the protective shell of familiarity and seek new sources of nurture.

Still working part-time at Gimbel's, I take on a volunteer job writing for the Mayor's Voluntary Action Center (MVAC) in Manhattan. In the beginning, my assignment sounds like a tall order: creating a brand new press kit describing the many outreach programs of the organization so that prospective volunteers and reporters will have information at their finger tips. I get to work, strongly motivated by the Center's confidence in my ability. I rewrite and update program descriptions, and design a new folder to hold them: Against a simple jigsaw background is the invitation "Let's Put It All Together," and the question, "Where do you fit in?" Later, I write the information blurbs about outstanding volunteers that will be read by Mayor Ed Koch at an upcoming Award Ceremony for Volunteers.

Still, the reality of entering my eighth year as a salesperson at Gimbels pricks my optimism somewhat. My personnel file shows that I've earned several glowing customer commendations. It records that I've been reprimanded for writing a letter to the company's president saying I find it demeaning, after several years of dedicated work, to be rewarded with a lapel pin emblazoned with the words "Professional Salesperson." The result of wearing it is more work: twice as many customers come to me instead of other salespersons on busy days. Why not a meaningful raise instead? An additional bit of paper in the file details my starting salary ($3.15 an hour) and what I make seven years later: five dollars and change an hour.

When someone at MVAC suggests I try my hand at a poster, I sit down and idly sketch a row of sprightly looking tulips because it will be spring soon. But I don't feel any ideas sprouting. I pencil in a couple of phrases like "Gain experience," "Learn new skills," and "Try out a new job." A moment later, I print "Let Yourself Grow!" across the bottom. Winifred Brown, MVAC's director at the time, comes up behind me and looking over my shoulder, exclaims with delight. "Oh, Ros, I love your slogan! Let's see if we can pair it with a graphic that has a more urban feel to it. This is going to become a `car card' that will go up in the city's subways."

She calls up a volunteer artist who knows how to make mechanicals. The artist designs a striking blue car-card featuring a New York-style skyline, and my slogan in white lettering. To my amazement, "Let Yourself Grow, Volunteer!" becomes the theme for MVAC's 1980 annual fundraising drive, used in radio, TV, and print ads as well as on the car-cards. As I board an IRT subway in mid-January, there it is in front of me, the first time I see the full-size car card. I smile, partly because I'm happy to have had a part in achieving this, but also because I know that it grew out of my talking to myself.

At first I'm very quiet when I decide to return to the Unitarian Church of All Souls at 80th and Lexington Avenue, where our children went to Sunday School when they were small. In this big urban church filled with highly educated and relatively wealthy members, I dread being judged by the clothes I wear, the way I look, the things I don't know. One Sunday a member of the Welcome Committee invites me to be a greeter, handing out programs as people arrive—instinctively, I cringe. I don't feel comfortable drawing attention to myself.

"Oh, I could never do that. I'm sorry." She looks surprised, I guess because that's a pretty easy way for returning members to help out and get to know people. I'm just not ready to stand out that much. Leaving behind one's protective covering – even that constructed in the mind – is hard to do. My long-time interest in social justice issues draws me instead to the Commission on Service, where I can feel less vulnerable and mostly work behind the scenes. On the first day of January, 1979, I write in my journal: "Last year was a good beginning...Working as a volunteer at MVAC has opened new doors already; I've felt that lovely burgeoning of new ideas that has so long been missing from my life... I've renewed friendships and reaffirmed my need for church as a source of inspiration and strength." As I write this, I have no idea that over the next fourteen years, All Souls Church will prepare me for deeper involvement in social action, and contribute greatly to my personal growth.

At first I attend every meeting, offer to write flyers, and help with programming. By 1980, the whole committee becomes increasingly concerned about how economic and social decisions are affecting the poorer neighborhoods around All Souls.

These are the Reagan years of building up a vast military arsenal and cutting social program budgets in order to pay for it. This creates vast funding deficits in the 'safety net' of organizations caring for the poor. In New York City, single room tenants are shaken out of their long-time lodgings; faced with steep apartment rents, many become homeless. Mental hospitals discharge patients who need to be monitored and require regular medication in order to function. Those without families end up on the streets. It is a wrenching time of watching civil society disintegrate, and questioning our power to do anything about it.

Slowly the Service Commission tries to decide how we can be most helpful to the community. But the burgeoning problems of homelessness and hunger seem far beyond our little group's capacity to remedy. We need to mobilize more volunteers, and work with groups outside our church. That fall, I present a Sunday morning workshop on voluntarism to a small group of members, based on my experiences at MVAC. It's one of a series organized by the Commission, culminating in a church-wide Volunteer Fair. The fair draws seventy people and invited speakers from several organizations. There is a lively question-and-answer session and each attendee receives a Volunteer Handbook that committee members have put together listing contact information for many more organizations. By 1981, I'm asked to become Chair of the Commission.

At first I don't give them an answer. I'm eager yet concerned about taking on this challenge, partly because I'm already struggling with another challenge: the onset of menopause and with it, an increase in the incidence and ferocity of my migraine headaches. I've suffered from them for twenty years. When the children were small, David would look after them while I took a strong pain-killer and lay motionless in the quiet back bedroom. A neurologist finally tested me in 1978, and said these headaches were a result of my taking one of the earliest, and strongest, birth control pills in1961. Some of the women who took them died of strokes. The new medicine he prescribes works well most of the time to get rid of the pain; I'm hopping with energy from the caffeine in it. Other days, I take it too late and must still shut myself away in a dark room, nauseous and miserable for hours.

Finally, despite reservations, I agree to be chair. I want to be part of the change that I know is coming. Early the next year, I think about how the Commission might best reach out to our counterparts in other religious institutions. Late one night I draft a letter to about twenty neighborhood churches and synagogues, suggesting that representatives from each of them meet with us to exchange ideas on community programs. That meeting becomes a launch pad for new programs, based on what is already working in some areas, and what might be accomplished with more participation. We begin to understand that hundreds, perhaps thousands of small groups like ours across the country are combining their energies in common purpose.

The sense of momentum is infectious, invigorating, and a little scary. Working with the Lenox Hill Neighborhood Association, All Souls becomes one of several churches agreeing to provide dinner and hospitality one night a week for a group of homeless women. Once the Board of Trustees' decision is made, our minister, Frank Forrester Church, appears in the pulpit the following Sunday and with quiet intensity puts forth "An Invitation to the Ministry." He explains that in times such as this, each one of us is called to be more than we think we can be. All of us can be ministers. After the service, fifty people crowd into our little meeting room to sign up. Once the homeless women's meal program is up and running, a few months later the All Souls soup kitchen starts providing lunch one day a week, requiring yet another set of volunteers because they are needed during the hours when many are working.

I'm downstairs at coffee hour one Sunday, when a young man I don't know walks up to me. He describes a petition started by the Quakers, which demands that the government declare a Nuclear Freeze—a Freeze that would put a stop to the unchecked building of enough bombs to annihilate the human race. I quickly realize he's doing exactly what our committee had done in a different area: enlisting as many church activists from other parts of the city as possible to work on getting petitions signed. "People all over the country are working on this. We hope to gather so many signatures Congress will have to listen to us."

The next Sunday, the Freeze petition is out on our activity table at coffee hour. Some people offer to take petitions and have people sign them at work. Others look mystified by the petition and say things like, "Don't you realize our country has to protect itself?" We keep the petitions out for weeks and talk about it with folks. I find myself at a sidewalk table on East 86th Street asking passers-by to sign. Eventually, pressure from ordinary people all over the United States succeeds in pointing out the dangers of amassing more and more nuclear bombs. Responding to huge national and international demand, Congress declares a freeze on their manufacture.

For months I'm so busy helping to plan events, enlist speakers, and organize meetings, that I barely have time to think about how I'm feeling. Yet there's been a quiet renaissance blossoming within me. When I finally find time for reflection, I hardly recognize who I've become: I am Rosalyn again – only with more experience and wisdom than before. The woman who had shunned visibility is now a respected member of the congregation, unafraid to speak from the lectern in the sanctuary, perfectly comfortable at a crowded information table during coffee hour. She's made wonderful new friends. And she is me.

Body

By the early 1980s, I feel compelled to seek at least minimal monitoring of my scoliosis; I've been doing some reading and worry that menopause may cause further weakening of my bones. This time, having switched HMOs, I see a new orthopedist. Lying uncomfortably on his exam table because of my curved spine, I describe my busy life, my hope that even though my scoliosis has gotten worse over the years, there must be something I can do to help myself. "What do other people like me do?" I ask him. "At your age, most of them don't do anything."

I bristle at his tone: What does he mean? That their lives are over anyway so what does it matter? Or that they've just given up because no one seems to know how to help them? I bite my tongue, say nothing.

After measuring my legs from my hip to the sole of my foot, he asks, "Did you know one of your legs is longer than the other?" "Yes," I say, "I have noticed that I seem to be somewhat off balance. I didn't know what to do so I've put felt heel pads in my left shoe for years but they wear out too quickly to be a good solution." I wait for him to suggest what needs to be done.

When his phone rings, I study the doctor as he wheels easily away from the exam table to answer it. He sits leaning slightly forward, legs apart, elbows on knees. I picture him out running at 5:30 A.M. or maybe chasing a racquetball with a friend. It's obvious he takes good care of himself. I've noticed the books on his desk that he has authored. He's probably an expert in many areas. But if I remember correctly, he got back on the phone again after he finished his exam, without providing any sort of help or advice to me.

Many years later, a physical therapist tells me my legs are actually the same length. During that time, because of what that doctor told me, I'd assumed I was in much worse physical shape than I actually was. According to the therapist, the scoliosis curve has caused one hip to be higher than the other, creating not only the illusion of a disparity in leg length, but also the very real need for a heel lift on my left side. She orders a permanent lift for my shoe. Whatever the cause of the difference, the doctor was certainly aware of it that day, but he allowed me to leave his office without so much as a prescription for a heel lift or an orthopedic shoe.

Around the time I've just about given up on orthopedists' expertise when it comes to dealing with scoliosis in later life, my older daughter has grown tall and willowy, with long, curly hair. She looks great, but doesn't feel well a lot of the time. Now in her early twenties, Lindsay finds she's allergic to wheat, eggs, and milk – all so basic, they're in everything. She begins to search for new ways to nourish herself. Listening regularly to radio talks by Dr. Ronald Hoffman, a well-known expert on nutritionally-based complementary medicine, and Gary Null, who encourages listeners to do their own research and ask questions, she scours libraries for food alternatives and new recipes; visits health food stores. Her investigation confirms what she has suspected all along: people have evolved over time thriving on plant-based, and other naturally-occurring, unprocessed foods – the opposite of the average American diet.

One sunny March morning, we're sitting at the dining room table. I'm making a grocery list while she chops veggies for aduki bean soup. I tell her I've noticed that on days when I eat more green vegetables, I have more energy. Squinting her eyes as she slices shallots, Lindsay replies, "Oh sure, food affects how we feel. Remember when I used to eat a candy bar or drink a soda and say it gave me a 'hot head'? Well, I wasn't crazy, though a couple of doctors thought I was. That was my body's reaction warning me I was sensitive to sugar, but I didn't understand it and neither did they." She starts dicing carrots and turnips. "And you, Mom, you should definitely avoid lots of sugar because it weakens the muscles and causes bone loss." When I hear this, I make a face. She must have noticed I have cookies on the grocery list. Would I have listened if a doctor told me to cut back on sugar? Maybe not. But no doctor ever did. Pouring the cascade of fresh veggies into the soup pot with the beans, Lindsay muses out loud, "It's been really empowering, digging to find what's out there about nutrition. The more I learn, the more strongly I feel it's up to an individual to be in charge of her own health!"

Lindsay slowly figures out how to change her diet, cooking for herself so she can minimize or avoid allergic reactions by eating rice and millet, root and green vegetables, and soy foods such as tofu. What she discovers ends up benefiting the whole family. My husband and I for years have been eating a typical American diet: lots of red meat like beef and ham; white bread; very few veggies; and generous amounts of sugary sweets. She and I begin to have long conversations about our being more open to trying to eat differently. I'm stuck in my old habits and resist at first; David would eat almost anything you put in front of him-- except sauerkraut. Finally we decide to try eating some healthier meals.

Over the next several years, we work at making change slowly. Our daughter makes delicious lentil soup. I learn to make pasta and beans with garlic and olive oil. We switch to whole grain bread, and eat more chicken and fish, very little beef. Swiss chard and asparagus start appearing on our table. David and I are amazed – we're moving into our fifties – and feel more energetic than we felt in our thirties.

That energy helps both of us to make decisions we'd been avoiding. Learning to be more assertive about my scoliosis teaches me to take control in other areas of my life: I leave Gimbels East after ten years and in 1983 take a fulltime job at the Council on Economic Priorities (CEP), a nonprofit public interest research organization. They are deeply involved in influencing corporations to be as innovative and generous in their community giving as they are in their business planning; to appoint more women and people of color to their boards and top officer ranks; and to closely monitor their activities with regard to environmental impact. At the time I join them, CEP is also urging congressional leaders not to support President Reagan's "Star Wars" space defense plan, which threatens the funding of social programs throughout the country. I'm eager to be part of CEP's social change work, because I've always felt that along with enjoying freedom, every American should share the responsibility of ensuring fairness and opportunity for all. Besides all these good things, I must confess—I look forward to working at a desk instead of standing behind a counter four hours a day.

David decides to retire a short time later after twenty-eight years at the National Board of the Young Women's Christian Association, the last fifteen years as research analyst. While there, he'd held several different positions in his union, a nonprofit chapter of AFSCME (American Federation of State, County, and Municipal Employees), including service on the negotiation team and chapter chairperson. During subsequent years he works for the nonprofit Center for Immigrants Rights, and takes courses at Cornell University to keep up to date on how national and international labor issues are being handled. Because his work life winds down slowly, it doesn't bother him that I'm still working. He worries sometimes that I'm working too hard, but he understands that I'm constantly learning and growing.

While Lindsay was researching nutrition, she also spent years looking into various unconventional ways to approach health problems -- ways that later have become widely accepted as conventional wisdom, but which in the late seventies and early eighties were still treated with skepticism by mainstream America, such as yoga, Reiki, acupuncture, and regular daily exercise. I'd begun to wonder: were there alternative therapies that might offer relief from the specific discomforts of scoliosis?

One evening in the early nineties, David and I are at an Upper East Side restaurant, quietly celebrating the end of a busy week. Putting a dollop of mashed potatoes into his chicken marsala sauce, he looks up at me with a grin. "How many years have we been sitting across from each other like this in restaurants? Must be thirty-five, anyway." I smile back, remembering. "And a lot of restaurants—first it was Child's in Pittsburgh, now we've got several favorites in New York." I squeeze lemon juice onto my broiled sole. "And you know what? We don't just eat good food; we usually have good talk when we eat out." The waiter brings us a basket of warm rolls and butter. "I have to say, Ros, I'm proud of you for taking on harder and harder things at CEP. You're doing the kind of research – measuring the effectiveness of programs and promoting social change -- that I wanted to do." Though his praise is sweet, my mind has been going in a different direction. It's been a hectic week, and I'm still feeling the effects of it. I tell him how it worries me that while I keep being given greater responsibility and am learning a great deal from the work, my energy level many days is quite low. At the same time, the stress level is intense. "I know what you mean," he says. "That's why I decided to give up that job at the Center for Immigrants Rights after four years."

"But I'm not thinking of quitting," I say, "I just need to find a way to feel better. Lindsay showed me a couple of ads this week -- not only are there alternative practitioners who give treatments for relaxation and energy-building, there's one who offers a treatment to help people with scoliosis. I was thinking of making an appointment with her soon." David tells me he thinks it would be a good idea and asks if I'd like him to go with me. Our eyes meet across the table and I think of all the support he's given me through the years, how fortunate I've been to marry him.

"I'd love that," I reply. Smiling, I feel the week's weight of tension lifting, knowing he's with me on this.

Soon after, we journey to Brooklyn to see a woman named Bea, who is a licensed massage therapist. Because she's had clients with scoliosis, Bea has devised a hot compress treatment that helps to relax taut muscles. For the next hour or so, as I lie on a padded table in her kitchen, Bea soaks soft towels in a big pot of steaming water, wrings them, and places them on my midsection in front, and in various places on my back. She leaves them on until they cool –and reapplies them newly heated several times. Little by little, I can feel the muscles unclenching and my whole midriff area seems more "opened out" than it has been in years. Will it last? When I stand up, will that feeling of space disappear?

The treatment isn't cheap; I ask her if I need to keep coming back. "Coming here for treatment is up to you. I'll give you a diagram of where the towels should go; you can heat water at home, and either you or someone else can apply the towels. It's more work, but you'll get the same result."

And so begins a year or so of keeping a hotplate and soup kettle on my bedroom chest of drawers, of putting down plastic to protect the varnished floor from dripping water, of trying to fit three or four hot compress treatments into a busy week. Lindsay helps much of the time so I don't need to jump up and reheat the towels myself. Over that time, there's a welcome change – I feel straighter, don't tire as easily, and even sleep better.

But my work begins to become more physically challenging. Whoever told me that people who work for nonprofits get to do everything certainly had it right; it's just taken me a while to understand what they mean. One day, I'm handling a big copy job, and am down on my hands and knees trying to figure out how to un-jam the copier for the third time. Or I need to get out a large mailing and wrestle with the ancient postage meter myself because the mail room person doesn't show up. The office switches from typewriters to computers, a difficult leap for me in my fifties. And I find that sitting long hours at a desk isn't necessarily a good thing for me or my scoliosis. Still, as I gain experience, I'm invited to speak to a Queens church group or Brooklyn YWCA conference about socially conscious buying and investing. Another day I consult with a representative of the Japanese firm for which I'm doing a study.

In my fourth year there, I get to do what I've longed for from the beginning: write an article for a national publication. When a senior writer and researcher finds he is too swamped with other commitments, I'm asked to write an article for *Ms. Magazine*. I'd written only newsletters before that, so jump at the chance. Basing my work on Steven Lydenberg's painstaking research, and incorporating updated material, I write "20 Companies That Listen to Women." I'm able to work with one of the best editors in the business. *Ms. Magazine* decides to make the piece its November 1987 cover story.

By this time, I often work overtime, either at the office or at home. Researching the social and ethical performance of companies is fascinating, rewarding, endless, and hard. I spend hours scouring annual reports and recent business articles; talking to unions, lawyers, and nonprofits about corporate records of labor problems and discrimination suits. I speak to people knowledgeable about the practice of `redlining,' to find out which banks deny loans to certain prospective borrowers. Details learned lead to more data to check, but deadlines are tight. The job involves pulling open packed file drawers at floor or shoulder level and lifting out heavy folders. On the days my body begins to knot up and ache, my brain loses focus by around three in the afternoon. I spend more 'sick days' at home, putting me farther behind in my work.

Reluctantly, I again seek out an orthopedist. But this time is different. Within ten minutes I know that here is a doctor who sees me in a way the others didn't. He doesn't cluck or sigh at my limitations. Instead, he considers my strengths.

"It's fortunate that you decided to forego the two operations back in the seventies. Your rib-cage has evolved in such a way that you actually have more breathing space than you did before. You've been saved from having more adverse pulmonary involvement because of that."

At last, good news about my body.

This doctor applauds my efforts to stay strong by taking daily walks, and urges me to start a regimen of light exercise, as well. What he doesn't say is that there's nothing any orthopedist can do for me now; having an operation at this time in my life would be dangerous and achieve only minimal correction. Over the last decade I've come to realize it's up to me now to take care of myself. But he's the first physician who has seen me as a successful, active person, not a casualty. I thank him, wondering whether he can see the tears in my eyes, and make my way home, smiling.

Now that Lindsay has been promoted at her accounting office, she and I both come home late and tired. It becomes too much trouble to keep using the hot towels. Deciding that exercise has to be an important next step, I briefly explore other alternatives: For a while I practice a few yoga exercises and later attend Feldenkrais classes, where we learn small, slow movements that incrementally retrain the brain and body to work together for improved flexibility and balance.

In the mid-nineties, I'm hard at work co-researching and writing a forthcoming book for the Council that will feature updated charts rating companies on social issues. In December, a series of snow storms make travel treacherous every weekend. As I leave for church one Sunday, there's a layer of ice just beneath the snow. My right foot slips forward; in trying to catch myself, my left foot goes backward. I go down hard and feel a tearing pain in my groin. David helps me stand and get back up the steps to the house, but alarm bells are going off. The pain is terrific, and the doctor won't be there today. I call the office anyway, describe what happened, and the doctor on emergency duty tells me to *apply heat* off and on for a couple of hours. I am in such a state that I do what he tells me to do. By the next day, I'm convinced there was internal bleeding and that I should have been advised to apply a cold pack. As a result, it takes weeks for me to heal.

I work at home on the book for a while, but there is lingering tenderness long afterward, so I stop doing any kind of exercises. Back in the office, the long days seem to eat up every speck of energy. When a friend from church calls and hears how exhausted I am, she urges me to come visit her. "I'll give you a treatment to loosen up the energy flow in your body. It will take a lot of that tiredness away." I suggest a day and time, realizing that she lives just two blocks from where I work.

Margery's apartment is calm and welcoming, a single lamp lit in the corner. She invites me to lie down fully clothed on a comfy cot, then places the fingers of one hand on the back of my neck and touches my ankle with the other. Quietly explaining what she will do and how it will help, she moves slowly from one area of my body to another, always touching two different places at once. She's practicing the ancient Japanese art of healing called Jin Shin Jyutsu, which I'd never heard of before. A little nervous at first, I wonder how light touching is going to coax away the tension straddling my shoulders, or get rid of the dull pain in my lower spine. As she works, I become aware of pleasant, unnamable ripples cascading intermittently within my body-- sometimes from hip to toe, sometimes from my upper body to my knees. At the same time, a pervasive sense of ease so relaxes me that I'm amazed when Margery wakes me after an hour and a half, asking me how I feel. The miraculous absence of tension is a gift when I need it most. I come back for months, using this method to help combat the effects of stress on my body and mind.

For some time now, Lindsay has been talking with David and me about quitting her job and using her savings to go back to school. It means that she'll continue living at home but will be preparing to use her skills and interests in the health profession, which makes perfect sense to us. While visiting a health fair at Riverside Church, she was advised to get a New York State license before practicing any kind of professional body work, so that is first on the list. Over the next decade, she attends the Swedish Institute for Massage and receives that license; earns a BA in Psychology from Hunter College; and completes the intensive series of courses required to become a Jin Shin Jyutsu practitioner. She'll be able to help others the way I've been helped by Margery, and I'll be able to have those same relaxing, energizing treatments at home.

Today, there are an increasing number of people taking a more active role in the management of their own health, educating themselves, questioning their physicians, opting more often for at least some treatment choices outside the mainstream. The internet is a great help, providing information to more people. But even before the internet, I was able to discover a universe of constructive, non-invasive help available to people like me. You will find some of these listed in the back of this book. None of this is free, but once learned, much can be done at home. I wonder how many people with longstanding scoliosis conditions might still be searching for answers? And how many give up because they're told by orthopedic surgeons that surgery is the only solution – and if you're too old for that, you're out of luck!

In May, 2007, I arrive with David and Lindsay at Northeastern University in Boston for the Fourth International Conference on Conservative Management of Spinal Deformities. This is the first conference of its kind in the United States, gathering together the most recent research about non-invasive treatment of scoliosis. And I am here, able to be a part of it. I've worked so hard to take care of myself; I'm expecting this day to be filled with reinforcement and revelation.

Joining the grandmothers, parents, and preteen children streaming into the large meeting room, it strikes me that we are a kind of family. All of us have a relative touched by scoliosis or have it ourselves. Though we don't know one another, we all know what it's like to watch a seemingly healthy spine begin to bend unnaturally. My warm feeling is pierced by the incontrovertible reminders of our commonality: I walk behind a young girl and her mother, each with a wayward spine that pushes out against her clothing below one shoulder blade. I'm looking at myself at fourteen and thirty-eight.

A subdued stir of movement and conversation fills the hall as we find places at long U.N.-like rows of tables, divided by a center aisle. Chairs are padded and comfortable. At each place, we find a pencil and fresh pad of notepaper along with a foil-wrapped chocolate in its fluted brown paper cup – the opening day of the conference is Mother's Day.

The doctors and researchers assembled onstage have come from Spain, Germany, Italy, Japan, Greece, and Poland, in addition to the United States and Canada, to talk about the subject uppermost in all our minds: Non-invasive treatment of scoliosis. The room settles into quiet. I savor the syrupy sweetness of my chocolate-covered cherry, feeling the imminence of history, a change in the very atmosphere. Finally, attention is being paid.

"Good morning! My name is Joe O'Brien. I'm President of the National Scoliosis Foundation and I am a person with scoliosis. I have a large family and several of them also have scoliosis... We gather here today to examine the intense work going on in many countries to establish a solid base of scientific support for non-invasive early treatments for scoliosis. With such support, children diagnosed with scoliosis will be offered physical therapy, carefully monitored exercise regimens, and if necessary, bracing, before resorting to surgery. Our distinguished speakers also will be stressing the importance of involving children and teenagers in what they themselves can do to strengthen their own bodies."

O'Brien's words take me back to the story of Katharina Schroth I'd found online a few months ago. Tears ran down my face as I sat before the computer, scrolling through the history of this woman born in Germany over a century ago. Diagnosed with scoliosis as a young teenager, Schroth had worked out her own regimen of intentional movement and something called "rotational breathing," both of which helped minimize the effects of her deformity. Later, she established a clinic and was successfully training children and teens how to cope with scoliosis – without surgery – when I was diagnosed in 1947.

My mind struggled to accept the reality presented on the screen: *The treatment likely to have helped me most did exist when I was seeking treatment. There was a third choice.* But it was unavailable to me. Doctors in the United States would not have been inviting experts from postwar Germany to share their views, especially now that surgery was more evolved (and lucrative) here. The orthopedist my mother and I consulted told us what was true in 1947, within the U.S. There were only two choices, bracing and surgery. I, and probably thousands of others, who could have been helped by learning the Schroth method, didn't know it existed.

As the speakers of the morning discuss bracing, I learn how differently this treatment is handled now than it was 60 years ago. Today, braces are adjusted or changed over growth years to allow for curve correction and normal growth. Thus, a patient might have three or four braces, while I wore the same one for four years. Most doctors nowadays view the rigid plastic braces of the seventies as antiquated because they were physically confining and might actually restrict breathing, causing some children to not engage in athletics at all.

One of the main reasons I've come to this conference is that Schroth's grandson, Dr. Hans-Rudolf Weiss, Medical Director of the Katharina Schroth Spinal Deformities Rehabilitation Center in Bad Sobernheim, is presenting demonstrations of his grandmother's pioneering therapy. I've read his 2006 study citing a disturbing sea-change that appeared in our country's approach to treating scoliosis – a change that began to evolve in the forties. Many U.S. clinics had recommended specialized exercises and/or surgery up until 1941. But that year, an analysis by the American Orthopaedic Association concluded that there was little difference, in terms of improvement, between surgery and exercise. What struck me about the facts revealed in Weiss' report was that after the 1941 study was published, the regular use of exercise to treat scoliosis for the most part disappeared in the U.S. Conversely, the use of surgery developed widely as the only choice if bracing was rejected or did not work. Why, I wonder? Was it simply money that impelled so many practitioners to move away from non-invasive exercises toward surgery, if results for each were roughly equal?

Dr. Martha Hawes, a research scientist at the University of Arizona in Tucson, is one of two women lecturers this morning. I hang on every word as she presents her own personal experience to make an important point: Diagnosed as a teenager with moderately severe scoliosis, she declined surgery, choosing to learn torso-strengthening exercises from a physical therapist. By her late forties, after continuing to use non-surgical therapies, she was able to achieve greater chest wall expansion, and a fifty-percent reduction in her curvature. Her 2003 book, *Scoliosis and the Human Spine*, documents extensive reliable research that shows the use of noninvasive treatment has the potential to lessen or end scoliosis.

It's hard to describe the range of my feelings this afternoon as I sit watching what, to me, is a miracle in process. We're in a large auditorium with successively higher tiers of seats like a concert hall. I'm down front in the second row, just a few feet from two therapists using Schroth exercises. One is doing breathing work with a girl about ten years old; another gently manipulates the body of a sixteen-year-old girl lying on a massage table. I learn that, in a person with a scoliotic curve, many muscles are involved. Some of them gradually stretch and grow thinner, others shorten. This process weakens the body's support system, creating muscle inequality and leading to changes in the body's shape. The Schroth method uses rotational breathing and physical therapy to strengthen and restore the balance of these muscles and help reduce rib humps.

I close my eyes, imagining I'm fourteen again, only this time I'm being taught how to help myself. I get impatient sometimes – the exercises aren't easy and I feel like I'm not doing them very well. But the therapist treats me like a grown-up. She tells me that by doing them regularly I can train my body to be stronger. That'd be great -- I want to be able to jump higher when I play basketball. I'm the tallest girl in gym class and everyone depends on me to make baskets. Feeling her gentle touch on my rib cage, I raise my arms and place my hands against the wall. I practice breathing in a different way: taking in more air on my lower right side, opposite the hump, than on the left. Then, at the therapist's urging, I focus on an area further up, breathing in more air on my left side, and less on the right. I listen as she tells me this therapeutic breathing will become an important part of my life; it will literally give me more space in which to breathe.

When I open my eyes, I'm back in my auditorium seat, far beyond youth and basketball, irretrievably bent -- not experiencing, but watching change. At seventy-three, I sometimes have trouble remembering how it felt not to be bent. Perhaps because there are children here today, my mind jumps to a time in third grade gym when we had to lie on our stomachs, reach back to grab our ankles, and rock back and forth. Being skinny made it easier for me; the overweight kids were having trouble. My spine was still normal even the winter I was thirteen -- I'd hurry out the school door, take a running start and slide all the way down the rutted, snowy hill to the street behind my house. How good that felt. I always did love to fly.

Now I inhale the hope alive in this room. In the young people who are part of the future. In the parents and grandparents whose eyes are being opened to treatments they hadn't even imagined. I focus again on the careful observation of each patient by the therapists, their movements sensitive both to what they see and what they feel. I've missed this miracle. I'm so glad the children haven't.

In a swaying Amtrak car headed back to New York the next morning, I recall something Martha Hawes said yesterday: When she was eleven, her surgeon told her that exercises wouldn't work, and even if they did, children wouldn't do them. She not only did do them, but understood early that she herself must search for other therapies that would offer her relief. That's what I'm trying to do.

Wings

Lunchtime chatter swirls around me in the busy coffee shop; disjointed conversations about the 2008 election and the high price of gas. I am in a different place, a quieter space. I stare out the window at the vertical 'Emergency' sign on the corner of the Mount Sinai Hospital of Queens across the street, remembering the April day ten years ago when the EMTs wheeled me out of an ambulance and into that hospital. The huge white letters on red loomed stark and frightening above me – I was the emergency. A cold drizzle pelted my face as they eased the gurney up onto the curb and through the double doors. Once inside the corridor and onto a freight-size elevator, I wished I were back out under that gray sky, walking to the grocery store, safe under my umbrella. The evening before, at a church retreat in upstate New York, I'd caught my foot behind a chair leg, and crashed to the tiled floor. I knew on the way down I was going to break something.

The orthopedic surgeon confirms that my right femur bone (hip) is broken and I'll need surgery to install a replacement. He tells me that when I'm a little stronger, I'll be transferred to the Hospital for Joint Diseases for a week of rehab. I nod, glad they're scheduling the operation for tomorrow morning. After he leaves, I think, soon the worst will be over. Or will it? They're going to implant a metal plate and screw in a bone I suspect is weakened by osteoporosis. Will my balance be better or even more off than it's been lately? I think my uncertain balance is probably the reason I've been falling so much. I just want my life back – I'll do whatever they tell me to do– even if it hurts.

Sometime after the anesthesia and pain pills wear off and hot pain shoots through my thigh when I move it, I remember that I'm supposed to be attending a writer's conference this weekend. Switching on the light for assistance, I think to myself, just roll with it—clear your calendar for the next few weeks. You're going to have to get used to being helped to the bathroom, to being unable to lie on your side at night. On the other hand, you're going to have about ten days doing nothing but swallowing pills and being punctured by needles, so maybe you can do a little writing while you're in here. As soon as I put my spiral notebook and pen on the adjustable tray table next to the water pitcher and box of Kleenex, I feel a lot better.

There are complications – I need a catheter for days because I'm unable to pass water. After several bouts of nausea at lunch time they realize that I'm allergic to the bladder retention medicine. But there are small victories, as well: two days after surgery, I'm happy to learn I can negotiate steps: step up with the good left foot, pull up the right. I surprise the aides when I climb up on the footstool and pull myself onto my high hospital bed instead of their having to lift me.

What I don't foresee is the heavy toll that hospital food, round-the-clock medication, and lack of exercise, takes on my body. Every morning I look out the window for rays of sunshine, but it's uniformly gray. One after another, the April days are all the same: lowering clouds, wind and rain. I find myself merely keeping a daily log in my notebook. I do crosswords, read, and go to therapy sessions. I don't write.

The hospital bed, however uncomfortable for prolonged habitation, has become my island – a small space of calm amid the bustle of activity. I do a lot of thinking here. I wonder how long it will be before I can deal with subway steps and crowds, enough to go back to work. I'm worried because there's no railing on our outside steps at home. And I feel as though the slightest puff of wind is likely to blow me over.

Why did this accident happen anyway? On the one hand, I know that as an older woman of European extraction, I probably must have osteoporosis, especially having had scoliosis to begin with. On the other hand, over the last few years I've fallen three times – twice on concrete – and never broken a bone.

Three years ago, in 1995, I asked to have a bone density test so I could make intelligent decisions according to what it showed about the state of my bones. I visited an endocrinologist because only with his approval would my HMO allow such a test. His exam found me in good health except for the scoliosis condition. I told him I was taking calcium and vitamins, exercising, walking, and using a hormone cream intended to strengthen bone, all of which he applauded. Then he asked me, if the test showed deterioration, would I go on estrogen therapy?. I answered with an emphatic "no" because I'd read articles written by both female and male doctors I respected who cited a serious risk of cancer. With an 'I know more than you do' smile, he said, "So then, what's the use of your having the test? I can't recommend you take it if you won't agree to the only treatment that will help you!"

We argued for an hour, I, thinking for a little while I could bring him around. I pointed out that the test would give me some idea of the condition my bones were in, which I didn't have now. With this information, I could seek out therapy designed to strengthen my skeletal structure. His absolute inability to give credence to my point of view made me furious; as my blood pressure rose, I knew the outcome of our discussion was inevitable.

Disgusted, I left his office, and never returned to him or that HMO. A few months later, when I sought the same test from a new doctor, he was evasive, saying no one had ever asked for one; and he would try to find out where I could get one. Two visits later, he still had no answers for me. I finally went back to the lone orthopedist who'd been perceptive and kind to me, over a decade before. He wrote a letter to my new primary doctor, saying "It is only good science to allow this patient, who already has a serious scoliosis condition, to be given a bone density test."

Within the next week, I had the test – two years after I'd first asked for it. While it showed the lumbar (lower) spine to be severely osteoporotic, the two femurs (hip bones) were judged moderately osteoporotic. Seven months later, I broke my hip. Would having the bone density test sooner have made a difference in this outcome? Perhaps. I would have had those two years to work at strengthening that part of my body.

Sighing, I plump up my pillows, wincing because leaning forward involves my thigh muscles. What shall I do about work? I'm not sure if I'll know who I am anymore if I'm not working. Writing and doing research for the Council on Economic Priorities offered a bumpy, unpredictable ride, but an amazing one. In the early nineties, I co-authored a series of "Shopping for a Better World" pocket guides to socially responsible companies, and two trade books about socially conscious buying and investing. I remember how rewarding recognition was: being invited to be one of the keynote speakers at a Women & Work Conference sponsored by the University of Texas (Austin); lecturing a class in International Business and Human Rights at Columbia University; addressing the Foundation for Public Affairs in Washington, DC. I became comfortable with press calls, enjoyed having my name in the newspapers once in a while. The Council is a demanding and fast-paced place to work and I've learned so much over the last fourteen years. But, do I really want 'demanding and fast-paced' anymore? I'm only a year away from retirement age; why not take this opportunity to retire early?

The next morning, my eyes barely open after a restless night, the idea sounds even better. David agrees when he comes to visit in the afternoon, pointing out that I'll begin to receive Social Security, anyway, but at a slightly lower rate than if I waited a year. After he leaves, one of the blue-uniformed aides pops in and says, "How would you feel about a shower and shampoo in the morning?" "Oh, lovely, I'll be back in the human race!" I go to bed early and sleep well.

The first few weeks back home, I practice regular stretching and exercise at a gym to build up the weakened parts of my body; I'm still on crutches but my old physical energy is coming back. Without the challenge of daily work, I feel at loose ends. Though I have a computer at home now and put in one or two days a week writing and editing for CEP, there isn't the challenge and satisfaction I knew when working on a book or researching information for our annual award dinner. More often than not, what I feel is bored. When I've finished the second library book I got that week, and plowed my way through countless crossword puzzles, what am I supposed to do? Especially if I remember that last week when I felt energetic enough to tackle some of my paper stacks, I tired quickly and had to stop in the middle. I'm not a TV-watcher; I like being busy and challenged -- but with what?

In May, shortly after leaving the hospital, I'd seen my daughter Julie receive her Phi Beta Kappa award from SUNY-Stony Brook. Sitting in the wheelchair she's thoughtfully arranged for me, I am so proud – our second daughter has weathered a divorce, raising her small daughter as a single mom; then later she remarried, all while fighting recurrent bouts of depression. It's taken her a long time to finish because life got in the way, but she's made it. A month later, our granddaughter, Melissa, graduates from high school. Julie and I sit down in front of the bleachers at the edge of Riverhead High's football field, her husband Bruce and David nearby. Julie's Dominican in-laws (from her first marriage) get stuck in traffic and arrive just in time to cheer as Melissa marches triumphantly up for her diploma. She's going to spend a year in Sweden as an exchange student and then will go on to college in San Diego.

The old longing begins to stir, a hunger in my gut that never goes away. I still want to go to college – not just a course here and there, but matriculating to earn a degree. What a gift that would be at this time in my life! Ah, but there are all the "buts:" I'll never be able to pass the math test to get in. Even if I could, my brain won't be able to wrap itself around subjects so much more advanced than my high school curriculum in the 1950s. And anyway, we can't afford it.

Two years pass. One February day, I find a mailing from CUNY Graduate Center in my box and sit munching a chicken and sprout sandwich while I glance through it to see what the new programs are. Almost buried in a sidebar, I spy an invitation to find out more about something called a CUNY BA. It's a new kind of degree – one that you can design yourself. I sit with the brochure in my hands and pray that this might be a way I can go back to school. The orientation meeting is in May; I plan to be there.

I stand in the long line of black-robed students six years later, hoping my mortarboard with the six strategically placed bobby pins will stay put in my thinning hair for a few more moments. There are 102 students in my class, most of them young, but gently seasoned with a few older ones like me. At 72, I am the oldest. It is June 5, 2006. Today I receive a CUNY Baccalaureate Degree after five intense years at Hunter College where my focus was Women's Studies. The line creeps forward slowly as Dr. Nan Bauer-Maglin, then head of the CUNY-BA program, reads from the cards detailing each student's achievement. I am proud to be in this company; there are so many high-achievers in the room. As I start up the steps, Nan smiles and calls out my name. She remembers me at the orientation seven years before, shyly asking questions about the program, worried already about the math requirement. I reach the stage and pause as she reads from my card: Rosalyn Will, Women's Studies, Summa cum laude, First Prize Memoir Contest, Dean's List. Thunderous applause buoys me as I walk across the stage and descend again to the auditorium floor. My four kids come running over to give me hugs— my incredibly "big" kids, ages 37 to 49, who all have managed to be here today. Walking up the aisle to my seat, where David waits with a congratulatory grin, people in the audience call out to me and some take my picture. I wish I could tell them that despite the hard work, this was a journey that always felt like a blessing.

Later that day, sitting quietly with my journal on my lap, I remember Nan coming to me before the ceremony began, asking if it was okay with me to stand up when she identified me as the oldest graduate in the class. How honored I felt that she thought this was important to recognize, and that she had spoken with me first about it. And I recall a middle-aged woman with sad eyes who came up to me in the hall afterwards. She read my face as though trying to memorize it. "You give me hope," she said. Holding her hand in both of mine, I wished her well. "So many people have helped me along the way. Let people help you." As my journal waits for me to describe this amazing day, I think long thoughts about how crowded life is with daunting challenges, not to mention the everyday stuff that steadily saps our energy. I'm convinced that many people would choose to keep on growing if they could find a way – and the help -- to do it.

Turning to a new page in my journal, I begin: I am so happy to have achieved this – and happier still to be able to continue – I've been accepted to the Memoir Master's Program in the fall. To write a memoir is a dream I've had for 20 years. The early twists and turns in my life, like those in my spine, were sometimes painful, but there has been so much more to living than that. All of it – the joys and achievements I've experienced and the unwelcome setbacks – were worth putting down, I felt. That conviction is what I described in my 2000 application letter to the CUNY BA program:

"I've read the journals of pioneer women and listened to the stories of attendees at the Women's International Writing Guild conferences in the 1990s, and they are the same stories. Women have always told each other stories, life lessons that have helped them struggle and compete and survive and excel. I would like to be one of those storytellers."

Now I can't wait to begin. It will all be there: Pittsburgh, my parents, the mentors who helped form me. The cloud of unhappiness that shadowed our family. The diagnosis of scoliosis at fourteen. The changes scoliosis will make in my life. I've begun many times before,

but this time I'll be learning how to do it better. And when I finish it –
this time I will finish it – it will have a happy ending.

Epilogue

I have always been good at visualizing: How to transform an ordinary room with warm colors, plants, an inexpensive rug or pair of drapes; how to put together a wardrobe of loose-fitting, attractive clothing from thrift shops. But this is different.

Now I'm being asked to breathe in a totally different way – carefully, intentionally – concentrating harder on this routine life activity than ever before. The Schroth-trained physical therapist, Marian Wade, and my daughter, Lindsay, stand nearby as I attempt rotational breathing for the first time. It is January 12, 2010.

In my mind is a vivid picture of the exhausted rubber ball that a young Katharina Schroth focused on and used as her inspiration a century ago: The old ball was deflated on one side, concave in appearance. But what if air was blown into that depression, she reasoned; then the ball would return to its proper shape and usefulness. She decided to direct her intake of air into the concave places in her body as a daily exercise, standing between mirrors, and saw that her rib humps slowly went down in direct proportion to the lessening of concavity. But she was a teen-ager at the time. Why do I think this will help my aging body, which has had more than sixty years to twist itself out of shape? I am sensible enough not to expect miracles, yet I have long believed in doing what I can to improve my physical quality of life.

I sit backwards on a wooden chair and have taken off my sweater so that my back is easier to view. Ms. Wade has indicated the hollowed place on my left lower back that I should focus on breathing air into. I remember watching the therapist at the 2007 Scoliosis Conference working with a ten-year-old on breathing -- at 76, will my brain and body be able to work together to perform an exercise I've never done? Blocking out everything else, I visualize my air intake as not routinely filling my lung cavity, but literally detouring to the lower left and being constricted elsewhere. As I breathe in, breathe out, seeing in my mind a slow change in the concave area, my daughter says she can see my lower back expanding when I breathe in. The therapist exclaims, "Yes, you're doing it!"

Yes! I think, taking a rest. Can I do this and the other exercises she recommends regularly and will it help? Time will tell. All I can do is try.

Acknowledgments

Early teachers are so important. I remember three of them here: Helen Boggs, who in fifth grade saw in me a small artistic spark and blew upon it; Leanore Allen, for introducing me to the idea of possibility; and Alberta Ellis, who sent a poem I'd written to the Pennsylvania School Press Association, where it won First Prize.

Thank you to mentors Winifred Brown, the Rev. Dr. F. Forrester Church, and Alice Tepper Marlin, who helped me make the transition from child care to self care through volunteer work and a new career, in my forties and fifties.

To Nan Bauer-Maglin, former Director of the CUNY Baccalaureate Program and Deputy Director Beth Kneller, my profound thanks for recognizing that, at 67, I truly hungered to continue my education, and helping to make that possible in countless ways. I am especially grateful to Hunter College MFA Professors: Louise De Salvo, who taught me the intricate math of writing memoir -- subtracting that which is not really necessary while adding the depth and artistry that invite the reader inside; Kathryn Harrison, who in workshop sessions kept after me to ask myself questions, make good use of constructive criticism, and not give up; Meena Alexander, in whose craft classes I read memoirs steeped in pain and beauty, and was encouraged to share those qualities in my own life story.

For the sturdy support of my family, there are no words to express my gratitude, especially my husband David, who remembered things I couldn't recall and helped so much with historical information. Eternal thanks to him and to our children, Lindsay, Julie, Eric, and Scott, for listening, reading, suggesting, and understanding when I needed to be immersed in my writing. I am indebted to Margaret Bailey, a family member I hadn't seen for fifty years, who kindly provided family lore I'd thought was forever lost. A warm thank you to Alison Green Will, my daughter-in-law, for designing the beautiful cover of my book, and to my son, Scott, for his gifts of computer help and website design.

The comforting lift of friends who cared about what I was doing has been a special gift. Heartfelt thanks to Mark de Solla Price, whose computer and publishing knowledge were essential to this work getting into print; and to Laurel Blossom, who lent her sharp editing skills at a critical moment. Hugs of gratitude to Phyllis Andrews, Vinny Allegrini, Sondra Brooks, and Doris Jeffrey, who read earlier drafts and offered moral support. And a very special thank you to Margery Johnston, who first introduced me to Jin Shin Jyutsu, the health-supportive blessing that has given me strength and energy through eight years of college studies and the writing of this book!.

Resources

Noninvasive Treatments for Scoliosis:

Schroth Physiotherapeutic Method for Deformities of the Spine: Devised by Katharina Schroth in Germany in 1921, this holistic system uses rotational breathing, physical therapy, and attention to the psychological needs of the patient. The Katharina Schroth Spinal Deformities Rehabilitation Centre is at Korczakstrasse 2, D-55566 Bad Sobernheim, Germany. **U.S.-based physiotherapists who have received Schroth training, alphabetically by state:**

CALIFORNIA

Beatriz Torres PT, 3380 St. Michael Drive, Palo Alto, CA 94306 Phone: 650-494-2359, E-mail: btorres3380@sbcglobal.net, Website: http://www.scoliosispt.net Bilingual English and Spanish.

ILLINOIS

Avis N Leung PT, 691 Plainfield Road, Willowbrook, IL Phone: 630-856-8200, E-mail: eddie-avis-mo@att.net

MASSACHUSETTS

Marc Moromarco (Doctor of Chiropractic), 3 Baldwin Green Common, Suite 204, Woburn 01801 Phone: 781-938-8558, E-mail: mmoromarco@comcast.net, Website: drmoromarco.com

Christine Sharkey PT, Cooley Dickinson Hospital, Rehabilitation Department, 30 Locust Street, Northampton, MA Phone: 413-582-2310, E-mail: Christine_Sharkey@cooley-dickinson.org

NEW YORK

Marian Wade MS, PT, Certified Schroth Therapist, Scolioasis, 50 Morningside Dr # 32, New York, NY 10025-1756 E-mail: scolioasis@hotmail.com Website: http://www.scolioasis.com Phone: 212-866-0648

OREGON

Cara Benton PT, Judy Trzebiatowski PT, Three Rivers Community Hospital, 500 Ramsey Ave., Grants Pass, OR 97527 Phone: 541-956-6225

VIRGINIA

Denise Bozue PT and Jennifer Graham PT, working with **Luke Stikeleather, Scoliosis Solutions,** 2802 Merrilee Drive, Suite 100, Fairfax, VA Phone: 703-849-9200

WISCONSIN

Beth Jannsen PT (1202 A Water Street), **Pat Orthwein PT** (1201 A Water Street), **Scoliosis Rehab Inc., Physical Therapy**, Stevens Point, WI 54481 Phone: 715-295-9820, Toll free: 877-734-2220, E-mail: info@scoliosisrehab.com, Website: www.scoliosisrehab.com

Sara Steffen PT, Rosan Zahn PT, St. Michael's Hospital, 900 Illinois Ave., Stevens Point, WI 54481 Phone: 751-346-5190

Cindy Marti PT, Amy Sbihli PT, Spinal Dynamics of Wisconsin, 2300 North Mayfair, Suite 555, Wauwatoso, WI Phone: 414-302-0770

Yoga:

Marcia Monroe PT, 161 West 15th St. 3A, New York City, NY 10011 marciamnro@aol.com

Yoga for Scoliosis: Elise B. Miller MA, a founding director of The Yoga Center in Mountain View, CA Private scoliosis sessions, workshops for practitioners. P.O. Box 60746, Palo Alto, CA 94306 Phone: 650-493-1254 E-mail: info@ebmyoga.com Web: www.yogaforscoliosis.com

Yoga Union Center for Backcare and Scoliosis, 32 West 28th Street (4th fl.), New York, NY Phone: 212-532-1512. **Co-Directors: Alison West**, 212-889-8643, yogaunion@nyc.rr.com and **Deborah Wolk**, 212-677-0064, dwolkYoga@gmail.com Workshops, classes, private lessons.

Learn More About Scoliosis and Noninvasive Treatments:

Martha C. Hawes, *Scoliosis and the Human Spine*. Tucson, AZ: West Press, 2006.

Christa Lehnert-Schroth, *Three-Dimensional Treatment for Scoliosis, A Physiotherapeutic Method for Deformities of the Spine.* Trans. Christiane Mohr, Alistair Reeves, Douglas A. Smith. 7th Edition. Palo Alto, CA: The Martindale Press, 2007.

National Scoliosis Foundation, 5 Cabot Place, Stoughton, MA 02072 www.scoliosis.org

Treatments To Ease Discomfort and Enhance Well-being:

Feldenkrais Method of Somatic Education: Retraining of mind and body to achieve better balance and overall well-being. Some practitioners are specially trained in working with scoliosis. Headquarters: 5436 North Albina Avenue, Portland, OR 97217. Phone: 800-775-2118

Jin Shin Jyutsu, Inc.: An ancient healing art from Japan which involves the placing of hands at certain points on the patient's clothed body. Frees energy for a renewed sense of well-being: Headquarters: 8719 East San Alberto, Scottsdale, AZ 85258. Phone: 602-998-9331

Sources

Hawes, Martha C. *Scoliosis and the Human Spine.* Author's Foreword. Tucson: AZ. West Press, 2006.

Henretta, James A., David Brody, and Lynn Dumenil. *America, A Concise History.* Vol. 2, p. 702, 732. Boston: Bedford/St. Martin's, 1999.

Lehnert-Schroth, Christa. *Three-Dimensional Treatment for Scoliosis, A Physiotherapeutic Method for Deformities of the Spine.* Trans. Christiane Mohr, Alistair Reeves, Douglas A. Smith. 7th Edition. Palo Alto, CA: The Martindale Press, 2007.

Lorant, Stefan, et al. *Pittsburgh, the Story of an American City.* Third Edition, p. 357. Lenox, MA: Kingsport Press, 1980.

National Scoliosis Foundation, 5 Cabot Place, Stoughton, MA 02072 www.scoliosis.org

Pennsylvania State Archives. *The "Great Depression,"* Record Group 47: "Records of the County Governments, Dauphin County Board of Assistance Unemployment Relief Records, 1931-1937".

http://www.docheritage.state.pa.us/

Weiss HR, Negrini S, Hawes M, Rigo M, Kotwicki T, Grivas T, Maruyama T, and members of the SOSORT (Society on Scoliosis Orthopaedic and Rehabilitation Treatment). "Physical exercises in the treatment of idiopathic scoliosis at risk of brace treatment – SOSORT consensus paper 2005." Scoliosis **1**:6 (2006).

About The Author

At the age of 67, Rosalyn Will decided to go back to school. In 2006, she earned a CUNY Baccalaureate degree through studies at Hunter College, at 72 the oldest in her graduating class. Her major was Women's Studies, which did not exist when she was of college age. Two years later, she received Hunter's MFA in Creative Non-Fiction. Rosalyn has written poetry all her life, and co-authored two books on socially conscious purchasing and investing for the Council on Economic Priorities. In this book, she tells her own personal story. A native of Pittsburgh, Pennsylvania, she has lived in New York since 1955. Rosalyn and her husband have four children.

For the latest information and to reach Rosalyn Will, please visit her website http://www.RosalynWill.com

Made in the USA
Monee, IL
17 January 2023

25457344R00111